FTCE Professional Educator
Teacher Certification Exam

By: Sharon Wynne, M.S
Southern Connecticut State University

"And, while there's no reason yet to panic, I think it's only prudent that we make preparations to panic."

XAMonline, INC.
Boston

D1446143

To obtain permission(s) to use the material from this work for any purpose including workshops or seminars, please submit a written request to:

XAMonline, Inc.
21 Orient Ave.
Melrose, MA 02176
Toll Free 1-800-301-4647
Email: info@xamonline.com
Web www.xamonline.com
Fax: 1-781-662-9268

Library of Congress Cataloging-in-Publication Data

Wynne, Sharon A.
    Professional Educator: Teacher Certification / Sharon A. Wynne. -2nd ed.
    ISBN 978-1-58197-695-3
    1. Professional Education.   2. Study Guides.   3. FTCE
    4. Teachers' Certification & Licensure.   5. Careers

Disclaimer:
The opinions expressed in this publication are the sole works of XAMonline and were created independently from the National Education Association, Educational Testing Service, or any State Department of Education, National Evaluation Systems or other testing affiliates.

Between the time of publication and printing, state specific standards as well as testing formats and website information may change that is not included in part or in whole within this product. Sample test questions are developed by XAMonline and reflect similar content as on real tests; however, they are not former tests. XAMonline assembles content that aligns with state standards but makes no claims nor guarantees teacher candidates a passing score. Numerical scores are determined by testing companies such as NES or ETS and then are compared with individual state standards. A passing score varies from state to state.

Printed in the United States of America

FTCE: Professional Educator
ISBN: 978-1-58197-695-3

Table of Contents

Great Study and Testing Tips!

What to study in order to prepare for the subject assessments is the focus of this study guide but equally important is *how* you study.

You can increase your chances of truly mastering the information by taking some simple, but effective steps.

Study Tips:

1. <u>Some foods aid the learning process</u>. Foods such as milk, nuts, seeds, rice, and oats help your study efforts by releasing natural memory enhancers called CCKs (*cholecystokinin*) composed of *tryptopha*n, *choline*, and *phenylalanine*. All of these chemicals enhance the neurotransmitters associated with memory. Before studying, try a light, protein-rich meal of eggs, turkey, and fish. All of these foods release the memory enhancing chemicals. The better the connections, the more you comprehend.

Likewise, before you take a test, stick to a light snack of energy boosting and relaxing foods. A glass of milk, a piece of fruit, or some peanuts all release various memory-boosting chemicals and help you to relax and focus on the subject at hand.

2. <u>Learn to take great notes</u>. A by-product of our modern culture is that we have grown accustomed to getting our information in short doses (i.e. TV news sound bites or USA Today style newspaper articles).

Consequently, we've subconsciously trained ourselves to assimilate information better in <u>neat little packages</u>. If your notes are scrawled all over the paper, it fragments the flow of the information. Strive for clarity. Newspapers use a standard format to achieve clarity. Your notes can be much clearer through use of proper formatting. A very effective format is called the <u>*"Cornell Method."*</u>

> Take a sheet of loose-leaf lined notebook paper and draw a line all the way down the paper about 1-2" from the left-hand edge.

> Draw another line across the width of the paper about 1-2" up from the bottom. Repeat this process on the reverse side of the page.

Look at the highly effective result. You have ample room for notes, a left hand margin for special emphasis items or inserting supplementary data from the textbook, a large area at the bottom for a brief summary, and a little rectangular space for just about anything you want.

3. <u>Get the concept then the details.</u> Too often we focus on the details and don't gather an understanding of the concept. However, if you simply memorize only dates, places, or names, you may well miss the whole point of the subject.

A key way to understand things is to put them in your own words. If you are working from a textbook, automatically summarize each paragraph in your mind. If you are outlining text, don't simply copy the author's words.

Rephrase them in your own words. You remember your own thoughts and words much better than someone else's, and subconsciously tend to associate the important details to the core concepts.

4. <u>Ask Why?</u> Pull apart written material paragraph by paragraph and don't forget the captions under the illustrations.

Example: If the heading is "Stream Erosion", flip it around to read "Why do streams erode?" Then answer the questions.

If you train your mind to think in a series of questions and answers, not only will you learn more, but it also helps to lessen the test anxiety because you are used to answering questions.

5. <u>Read for reinforcement and future needs.</u> Even if you only have 10 minutes, put your notes or a book in your hand. Your mind is similar to a computer; you have to input data in order to have it processed. *By reading, you are creating the neural connections for future retrieval.* The more times you read something, the more you reinforce the learning of ideas.

Even if you don't fully understand something on the first pass, *your mind stores much of the material for later recall.*

6. <u>Relax to learn so go into exile.</u> Our bodies respond to an inner clock called biorhythms. Burning the midnight oil works well for some people, but not everyone.

If possible, set aside a particular place to study that is free of distractions. Shut off the television, cell phone, and pager and exile your friends and family during your study period.

If you really are bothered by silence, try background music. Light classical music at a low volume has been shown to aid in concentration over other types. Music that evokes pleasant emotions without lyrics is highly suggested. Try just about anything by Mozart. It relaxes you.

7. <u>Use arrows not highlighters</u>. At best, it's difficult to read a page full of yellow, pink, blue, and green streaks. Try staring at a neon sign for a while and you'll soon see that the horde of colors obscure the message.

A quick note, a brief dash of color, an underline, and an arrow pointing to a particular passage is much clearer than a horde of highlighted words.

8. <u>Budget your study time</u>. Although you shouldn't ignore any of the material, *allocate your available study time in the same ratio that topics may appear on the test.*

Testing Tips:

1. Get smart, play dumb. Don't read anything into the question. Don't make an assumption that the test writer is looking for something else than what is asked. Stick to the question as written and don't read extra things into it.

2. Read the question and all the choices *twice* before answering the question. You may miss something by not carefully reading, and then re-reading both the question and the answers.

If you really don't have a clue as to the right answer, leave it blank on the first time through. Go on to the other questions, as they may provide a clue as to how to answer the skipped questions.

If later on, you still can't answer the skipped ones . . . ***Guess.*** The only penalty for guessing is that you *might* get it wrong. Only one thing is certain; if you don't put anything down, you will get it wrong!

3. Turn the question into a statement. Look at the way the questions are worded. The syntax of the question usually provides a clue. Does it seem more familiar as a statement rather than as a question? Does it sound strange?

By turning a question into a statement, you may be able to spot if an answer sounds right, and it may also trigger memories of material you have read.

4. Look for hidden clues. It's actually very difficult to compose multiple-foil (choice) questions without giving away part of the answer in the options presented.

In most multiple-choice questions you can often readily eliminate one or two of the potential answers. This leaves you with only two real possibilities and automatically your odds go to Fifty-Fifty for very little work.

5. Trust your instincts. For every fact that you have read, you subconsciously retain something of that knowledge. On questions that you aren't really certain about, go with your basic instincts. **Your first impression on how to answer a question is usually correct.**

6. Mark your answers directly on the test booklet. Don't bother trying to fill in the optical scan sheet on the first pass through the test.
Just be very careful not to miss-mark your answers when you eventually transcribe them to the scan sheet.

7. Watch the clock! You have a set amount of time to answer the questions. Don't get bogged down trying to answer a single question at the expense of 10 questions you can more readily answer.

THIS PAGE BLANK

Competency 1.0   Knowledge of various types of assessment strategies that can be used to determine student levels and needs.

Skill 1.1 Identify measurement concepts, characteristics, and uses of norm-referenced, criterion-referenced, and performance-based assessments.

In evaluating school reform for school communities, educators may implement and assess student academic performance using a variety of factors including: norm-referenced, criterion-referenced, and performance-based assessments.

Effective classroom assessment can provide educators with a wealth of information on student performance as well as teacher instructional practices. Student assessment can provide teachers with the data needed to analyze student academic performance and make inferences about the effectiveness of student learning plans, which can foster increased academic achievement and success for students.

Assessment

The process of collecting, quantifying and qualifying student performance is defined as assessment. A comprehensive assessment system must include a diversity of assessment tools such as norm-referenced, criterion-referenced, performance-based, or student generated alternative assessments which can measure specific learning outcomes or goals for student achievement.

Norm-referenced Assessments
Norm-referenced tests (NRT) are used to classify student learners for homogenous groupings based on ability levels or basic skills into a ranking category. In many school communities, NRTs are used to classify students into AP (Advanced Placement), honors, regular or remedial classes that can significantly impact student future educational opportunities or success. NRTs are also used by national testing companies such as Iowa Test of Basic Skills (Riverside), Florida Achievement Test (McGraw-Hill) and other major test publishers to test a national sample of students which are used to develop norms against standard test-takers. Stiggins (1994) states "Norm-referenced tests (NRT) are designed to highlight achievement differences between and among students to produce a dependable rank order of students across a continuum of achievement from high achievers to low achievers."

Educators may use the information from NRTs to provide students with academic learning that accelerates student skills from the basic level to higher skill applications and thereby able to meet the requirements of state assessments and/or core subject expectations. NRT ranking ranges from 1-99 with 25% of students scoring in the lower ranking of 1-25 and 25% of students scoring in the higher ranking of 76-99. Florida uses a variety of NRTs for student assessments that range from Iowa Basic Skills Testing to California Battery Achievement testing to measure student learning in reading and math..

Criterion-referenced Assessments

Criterion-referenced assessments examine specific student learning goals and performance compared to a norm group of student learners. According to Bond (1996) "Educators or policy makers may choose to use a Criterion-referenced test (CRT) when they wish to see how well students have learned the knowledge and skills which they are expected to have mastered." Many school districts and state legislation use CRTs to ascertain whether schools are meeting national and state learning standards. The latest national educational mandate of "No Child Left Behind" (NCLB) and Adequate Yearly Progress (AYP) use CRTs to measure student learning, school performance, and school improvement goals as structured accountability expectations in school communities. CRTs are generally used in learning environments to reflect the effectiveness of curriculum implementation and learning outcomes.

Performance-based Assessments

Performance-based assessments are currently being used in a number of state testing programs to measure the learning outcomes of individual students in subject content areas. Washington state uses performance-based assessments for the WASL (Washington Assessment of Student Learning) in reading, writing, math and science to measure student-learning performance. Attaching a graduation requirement to passing the required state assessment for the class of 2008 has created high-stakes testing and educational accountability for both students and teachers in meeting the expected skill based requirements for 10th grade students taking the test.

In today's classrooms, performance-based assessments in core subject areas must have established and specific performance criteria that start with pre-testing in the subject area and maintaining of daily or weekly testing to gauge student progress towardlearning goals and objectives. To understand a student's learning is to understand how a student processes information. Effective performance assessments will show the gaps or holes in student learning which allows for an intense concentration on providing fillers to bridge non-sequential learning gaps. Typical performance assessments include oral and written student work in the form of research papers, oral presentations, class projects, journals, student portfolio collections of work, and community service projects.

Summary

With today's emphasis on student accountability, the public and legislature demands for effective teaching and assessment of student learning outcomes will remain of utmost importance. In 1994, thirty-one states use NRTs for student assessments, while thirty-three states use CRTs in assessing student learning outcomes (Bond, 1996).

Performance-based assessments are being used in some areas in the state testing of high school students. Before a state, district, or school community can determine which type of testing is the most effective, there must be a determination of testing outcome expectation, content learning outcome, and a decision as to the effectiveness of the assessment in meeting these learning goals and objectives.

Skill 1.2 Interpret assessment data (e.g., screening, progress monitoring, diagnostic) to guide instructional decisions.

The information contained within student records, teacher observations and diagnostic testing reports is only as valuable as the individual teacher's ability to comprehend the information. Although the student's cumulative record will contain some or all of this information, it is the responsibility of each teacher to read and interpret the information.

Diagnostic test results are generally uniform and may be easier to interpret. These reports usually include a scoring guide which tells the teacher how to interpret the information. Teachers should also realize that the scores should be interpreted with some caution as there are always uncontrollable factors, and therefore, test scores alone cannot be the ultimate indicator of a child's ability or learning needs. Many other factors influence these scores including: the rapport the child had with the tester, how the child was feeling when the test was administered, and how the child regarded the value or importance of the test. Therefore, the teacher should regard these scores as a *ball park* figure.

When a teacher reads another teacher's observations, it is important to keep in mind that each person brings to an observation certain biases. The reader may also influence the information contained within an observation with his/her own interpretation. When using teacher observations as a basis for designing learning programs, it is necessary to be aware of these shortcomings.

Student records may provide the most assistance in guiding instruction. These records contain information that was gathered over a period of time and may show student growth and progress. They may also contain information provided by several people including: teachers, parents, and other educational professionals. By reading this compilation of information the teacher may get a more accurate understanding of a student's needs. All of this information is only a stepping-stone in determining how a child learns, what a child knows, and what a child needs to know to further his/her education.

Skill 1.3 Identify appropriate methods, strategies, and evaluation instruments for assessing student levels, needs, performance, and learning.

Assessment language has been deeply rooted in key terms such as the following:

- *Formative*-sets targets for student learning and creates an avenue to provide data on whether students are meeting the targets
- *Diagnostic testing*- is used to determine students; skill levels and current knowledge
- *Normative*-establishes rankings and comparatives of student performances against an established norm of achievement.
- *Alternative*-non-traditional method of helping students construct responses to problem-solving
- *Authentic*-real life assessments that are relevant and meaningful in a student's life. (For example, calculating a 20% discount on a Texas Instrument calculator, for a student learning math percentages creates a more personalized approach to learning).
- *Performance based*-judged according to pre-established standards
- *Traditional*-diversity of teacher assessments that either come with the textbooks or ones that are directly created from the textbooks.

Using Assessment to Adjust Instruction
Assessment skills should be an integral part of teacher training. Teachers need to: be able to monitor student learning using pre and post assessments of content areas; analyze assessment data in terms of individualized support for students and instructional practice for teachers; and design lesson plans that have measurable outcomes and definitive learning standards. Assessment information should be used to provide performance-based criteria and academic expectations for all students in evaluating whether students have learned the expected skills and content of the subject area.

For example in an Algebra I class, teachers can use assessment to see whether students have acquired enough prior knowledge to engage in the subject area. If the teacher provides students with a pre-assessment on algebraic expression and can then ascertain whether the lesson plan should be modified to include a pre-algebraic expression lesson unit to refresh student understanding of the content area, then the teacher can create if needed, quantifiable data to support the need of additional resources to support student learning. Once the teacher has taught the unit on algebraic expression, a post assessment test can be used to test student learning and a mastery exam can be used to test how well students understand and can apply the knowledge to the next unit of math content learning.

Teachers can use assessment data to inform and impact instructional practices by making inferences on teaching methods and gathering clues for student performance. By analyzing the various types of assessments, teachers can gather more definitive information on projected student academic performance. Instructional strategies for teachers would provide learning targets for student behavior, cognitive thinking skills, and processing skills that can be employed to diversify student learning opportunities.

One of the simplest most efficient ways for the teacher to get to know his/her students is to conduct an entry survey. This is a record that provides useful background information about the students as they enter a class or school. Collecting information through an entry survey will provide valuable insights into a student's background knowledge and experience. Teachers can customize entry surveys according to the type of information considered valuable to them individually. Some of the information that may be incorporated include: student's name and age, family members, health factors, special interests, strengths, needs, fears, etc., parent expectations, languages spoken in the home, what the child likes about school, etc.

At the beginning of each school term the teacher will likely feel compelled to conduct some informal evaluations in order to obtain a general awareness of his/her students. These informal evaluations should be the result of a learning activity rather than a traditional testing format and may include classroom observations, collections of reading and writing samples, and notations about the students' abilities as demonstrated by classroom discussions and participation including the students' command of language. The value of these informal evaluations cannot be underestimated. These evaluations, if utilized effectively, will drive instruction and facilitate learning.

After initial informal evaluations have been conducted and appropriate instruction implemented, teachers will need to fine tune individual evaluations in order to provide optimum learning experiences. Some of the same types of evaluations can be used on an ongoing basis to determine individual learning needs as were used to determine initial general learning needs.

It is somewhat more difficult to choose an appropriate evaluation instrument for elementary-aged students than for older students. Therefore, teachers must be mindful of developmentally appropriate instruments. At the same time, teachers must be cognizant of the information that they wish to attain from a specific evaluation instrument. Ultimately, these two factors—students' developmental stage and the information to be derived—will determine which type of evaluation will be most appropriate and valuable. There are few commercially designed assessment tools that will prove to be as effective as the tool that is constructed by the teacher.

A simple-to-administer, information-rich evaluation of a child's reading strengths and weaknesses is the running reading record. "This technique for recording reading behavior is the most insightful, informative, and instructionally useful assessment procedure you can use for monitoring a child's progress in learning to read," (Traill, 1993). The teacher uses a simple coding system to record what errors and strategies a child uses while reading text out loud. At a later time, the teacher can go back to the record and assess what the child knows about reading and what the teacher still needs to address in an effort to help the student become a better reader.

If the teacher is evaluating a child's writing, it is a good idea to discourage the child from erasing his/her errors and to train the child to cross out errors with a single line so that the teacher can see the process that the student used throughout a writing assignment. This writing becomes an important means of getting to know about students' writing and is an effective, valuable writing evaluation.

Mathematics skills can be evaluated informally by observing students as they work at their seats or perform calculations at the board. Teachers can see if the students know basic computation skills, if they understand place value, or if they transpose numbers simply by watching them as they solve computation problems. Some teachers may prefer to administer some basic computation tests to determine a student's mathematical strengths and weaknesses. Although these methods are not as effective or thorough in assessing students, they are quick and easy to administer.

Skill 1.4 Identify and sequence learning activities that support study skills and test-taking strategies.

Tests are essential instructional tools. They can greatly influence students' learning and should be given due regard for the importance during preparation. Several studies have been carried out which indicate conclusively that students perform better when they understand what type of test they are going to take and why they are taking the test before they take it. If students perceive a test to be important or to have relative significance, they will perform better. In a recent study, students who were informed by their teachers as to how their test scores were to be used and who were also urged by their teachers to put forth their best effort scored higher on the Differential Aptitudes Test than students who did not receive this coaching.

Motivation to perform well on tests begins with the student. The intrinsic motivation is an internal drive by the student who aspires to do his/her best in school. The extrinsic motivation may be as simple as a student wanting to learn a basic mathematical skill to complete a remedial math class or as complex as a student needing to pass a Pre-Calculus class to take an AP (Advanced Placement) Calculus class during his senior year to gain college credit and enter University as an early college admission's applicant.

It is also a recognized fact that students will attain higher test scores if they are familiar with the format of the test. It is important for the student to know whether s/he will be taking a multiple-choice test or an essay test. Being prepared for a specific test format can enhance performance. Teachers can help students' boost their test performance by providing them with explicit information in regard to the content of the test.

If the focus is on improving student performance on tests, then students must become familiar with the diversity of test taking formats. Students must understand that there are basic study skills and preparations which maximize student outcomes.

In researching the effects of sleep deprivation on student learning and test-taking, Carlyle Smith, a professor of psychology at Trent University in Ontario determined that when students are taught a complex logic game of memorization, their performance on the logic game decreased by 30% when the students were in a sleep deprived state on the first night. In testing a second group of volunteers who had been deprived of sleep on a second night and another group given a full three nights rest, the results were similar in that their performance on the logic game was similar. For students, the best performance for test taking begins with a good night's sleep.

Effective test taking includes an ability to size up testing formats and quickly eliminate incorrect answers from a listing of possible choices. The good news is that a student has a 25% chance of getting the correct answer from a choice of four answers and a 50% chance once the decoys and incomplete answers have been eliminated to the final two answers remaining. Imagine two answers with a 50% chance of choosing the correct one. The odds are better if you can get the choices down to the last two remaining answer choices. Knowing how the test is constructed will get a student those better odds.

Objective Tests

Most objective tests will include multiple-choice questions, matching, and true/false questions that include a selection of answer choices. The correct answer can be found using a simple process of elimination of decoy of incomplete answers. Helping students review material needed for the tests and providing them sample practice questions will increase student-testing performance. Listed below are basic strategies for taking multiple choice tests such as the SAT, ACT, state tests and class assessment:

- Read the questions and the answers thoroughly.
- Look for decoy or partial answers and eliminate them
- Make an educated guess from the answers that remain
- For true/false answers, if any part of the answer given is false, then the entire answer is false, so you have a 50-50 chance of getting a correct response from true/false
- Answer the easy questions first and spend more time on the harder questions.
- Listen to your gut instinct on tests; usually your first instinct is correct, but don't be afraid to second guess your gut if you know for a fact that part of the answer that you've chosen has a false component embedded in the answer.

Subjective tests

Subjective tests put the student in the driver's seat. These types of assessments usually consist of short answer, longer essays or problem solving that involves critical thinking skills requiring definitive proof from the short reading passages to support your answer. Sometimes teachers provide rubrics that include assessment criteria for high scoring answers and projects. The bottom line is studying and preparing for any type of tests will equate to better student performance and achievement on tests.

Competency 2.0 **Knowledge of effective communication with students, parents, faculty, other professionals, and the public, including those whose home language is not English**

Skill 2.1 Identify appropriate techniques for leading class discussions (e.g., listening, identifying relevant information, probing, drawing inferences, summarizing student comments, and redirecting).

The major teaching functions include getting the class under way, providing instruction about what to complete, developing the lesson, managing seat work, homework, practice, and conducting reviews. All of the functions require teachers to comprehend the aptitude and achievement of students, the appropriateness of subject matter, and the kinds of difficulties students may encounter as they try to learn.

Engaging Students in Lessons:
Students' attitudes and perceptions about learning are the most powerful factors influencing academic focus and success. When instructional objectives center on students' interests and are relevant to their lives, effective learning occurs.

Learners must believe that the tasks that they are being asked to perform have some value and that they have both the ability and resources to perform them. If a student believes a task is unimportant, s/he will not put much effort into it. Additionally, if a student thinks he lacks the ability or resources to successfully complete a task, even attempting the task becomes too great a risk. Not only must the teacher understand the students' abilities and interests, s/he must also help students develop positive attitudes and perceptions about learning tasks.

Teachers can enhance student motivation by planning and directing interactive, "hands-on" learning experiences. Research substantiates that cooperative group projects decrease student behavior problems and increase student on-task behavior. Students who are directly involved with learning activities are more motivated to complete a task to the best of their ability.

Students generally do not realize their own abilities and frequently lack self-confidence. Teachers can instill positive self-concepts in children and thereby enhance their innate abilities by providing certain types of feedback. Such feedback includes attributing students' successes to their effort and specifying what the student did that produced the success. Qualitative comments influence attitudes more than quantitative feedback such as grades.

Despite a teacher's best efforts to provide important and appropriate instruction, there may be times when a teacher is required to teach a concept, skill, or topic that students may perceive as trivial and irrelevant. These tasks can be effectively presented if the teacher exhibits a sense of enthusiasm and excitement about the content. Teachers can help spark the students' interest by providing anecdotes and interesting digressions. **Research indicates that as teachers become significantly more enthusiastic, students exhibit increased on-task behavior.**

Teachers must avoid teaching tasks that fit their own interests and goals and design activities that address the students' concerns. In order to do this, it is necessary to find out about students and to have a sense of their interests and goals. Teachers can do this by conducting student surveys and simply by questioning and listening to students. Once this information is obtained the teacher can link students' interests with classroom tasks.

Student Responses:
Teachers are learning the value of giving assignments that meet the individual abilities and needs of students. After instruction, discussion, questioning, and practice have been provided, rather than assigning one task to all students— teachers are asking students to generate tasks that will show their knowledge of the information presented. Students are given choices and thereby have the opportunity to demonstrate more effectively the skills, concepts, or topics that they as individuals have learned. It has been established that student choice increases student originality, intrinsic motivation, and higher mental processes.

Various studies have shown that learning is increased when the teacher acknowledges and amplifies the student responses. Additionally, this can be even more effective if the teacher takes one student's response and directs it to another student for further comment. When this occurs, the students acquire greater subject matter knowledge. This is due to a number of factors.

One is that the student feels that he or she is a valuable contributor to the lesson. Another is that all students are forced to pay attention because they never know when they will be called on: group-alert. **The teacher achieves group alert by stating the question, allowing for a pause for the students to process the question and formulate an answer, and then calling on someone to answer.** If the teacher calls on someone before stating the question, the rest of the students tune-out because they know they are not responsible for the answer. Teachers are advised to also alert the non-performers to pay attention because they may be called on to elaborate on the answer. Non-performers are defined as all the students not chosen to answer.

The idea of directing the student comment to another student is a valuable tool for engaging the lower achieving student. **If the teacher can illicit even part of an answer from a lower-achieving student and then move the spotlight off of that student onto another student, the lower achieving student will be more likely to engage in the class discussion the next time.** This is because they were not put "on the spot" for very long and they successfully contributed to the class discussion.

Additionally, the teacher shows acceptance and gives value to student responses by acknowledging, amplifying, discussing or restating the comment or question. If you allow a student response, even if it is blurted out, you must acknowledge the student response and tell the student the quality of the response.

For example: The teacher asks, "Is chalk a noun?" During the pause time a student says, "Oh, so my bike is a noun." Without breaking the concentration of the class, the teacher looks to the student, nods and then places his or her index finger to the lips as a signal for the student not to speak out of turn and then calls on someone to respond to the original question. If the blurted out response is incorrect or needs further elaboration, the teacher may just hold up his or her index finger as an indication to the student that the class will address that in a minute when the class is finished with the current question.

A teacher acknowledges a student response by commenting on it. For example, the teacher states the definition of a noun, and then asks for examples of nouns in the classroom. A student responds, "My pencil is a noun." The teacher answers, "Okay, let us list that on the board." By this response and the action of writing "pencil" on the board, the teacher has just incorporated the student's response into the lesson.

A teacher may also amplify the student response through another question directed to either the original student or to another student. For example, the teacher may say, "Okay", giving the student feedback on the quality of the answer, and then add, "What do you mean by "run" when you say the battery runs the radio?"

Another way of showing acceptance and value of student response is to discuss the student response. For example, after a student responds, the teacher would say, "Class, let us think along that line. What is some evidence that proves what Susie just stated?"

And finally, the teacher may restate the response. For example, the teacher might say, "So you are saying, the seasons are caused by the tilt of the earth. Is this what you said?"

Therefore, a teacher keeps students involved by the utilization of group-alert. Additionally, the teacher shows acceptance and value of student responses by acknowledging, amplifying, discussing or restating the response. This contributes to maintaining academic focus.

The reason for praise in the classroom is to increase the desirable and eliminate the undesirable. This refers to both conduct and academic focus. It further states that effective praise should be authentic, it should be used in a variety of ways, and it should be low-keyed. Academic praise is a group of specific statements that give information about the value of the response or its implications. For example, a teacher using academic praise would respond, "That is an excellent analysis of Twain's use of the river in Huckleberry Finn." Whereas a simple positive response to the same question would be: "That's correct."

The focus of the classroom discussion should be on the subject matter and controlled by teacher-posed questions. When a student response is correct, it is not difficult to maintain academic focus. However, when the student response is incorrect, this task is a little more difficult. The teacher must redirect the discussion to the task at hand, and at the same time not devalue the student response. It is risky to respond in a classroom.

Redirecting Student Comments;
If a student is ridiculed or embarrassed by an incorrect response, the student may shut down and not participate thereafter in classroom discussion. One way to respond to the incorrect answer is to ask the child, "Show me from your book why you think that." This gives the student a chance to correct the answer and redeem himself or herself.

Another possible response from the teacher is to use the answer as a non-example. For example, after discussing the characteristics of warm-blooded and cold-blooded animals, the teacher asks for some examples of warm-blooded animals. A student raises his or her hand and responds, "A snake." The teacher could then say, "Remember, snakes lay eggs; they do not have live birth. However, a snake is a good non-example of a mammal."

The teacher then draws a line down the board and under a heading of "non-example" writes "snake." This action conveys to the child that even though the answer was wrong, it still contributed positively to the class discussion. Notice how the teacher did not digress from the task of listing warm-blooded animals, which in other words is maintaining academic focus, and at the same time allowed the student to maintain dignity.

It is more difficult for the teacher to avoid digression when a student poses a non-academic question. For example, during the classroom discussion of Romeo and Juliet, the teacher asks "Who told Romeo Juliet's identity?" A student raises his or her hand and asks, "May I go to the rest room?" The teacher could respond in one of two ways. If the teacher did not feel this was a genuine need, he or she could simply shake his or her head no while repeating the question, "Who told Romeo Juliet's identity?"

If the teacher felt this was a genuine need and could not have waited until a more appropriate time, he or she may hold up the index finger indicating "*just a minute*," and illicit a response to the academic question from another student. Then, during the next academic question's pause-time, the teacher could hand the student the bathroom pass.

Using hand signals and body language to communicate with one student while still talking to the rest of the class demonstrates effective teacher *with-it-ness*. *With-it-ness* is the behavior that demonstrates to the students that the teacher knows what s/he is doing. More specifically, in this case it is overlapping with-it-ness. This is the ability to do two tasks at once. Moreover, it is maintaining academic focus with the class while attending to the needs of the one student who needs to use the rest room or go to the clinic. During the academic day, many non-academic tasks need to be attended to. If the students learn early on that the teacher is not sidetracked by these interruptions, they will stay on task and greater subject matter acquisition will occur.

The teacher may opt to ignore questions that are posed to throw the class off-task. For example, in response to an academic question the student asks, "What time does the bell ring?" The teacher may respond by shaking his or her head no and calling on someone else to answer the academic question. Under no circumstances should the student posing the non-academic question be given an answer. Otherwise, this is rewarding deviant behavior and will result in a loss of academic focus.

Therefore, a teacher can ignore or redirect digressions without devaluing student responses by allowing the student to correct the answer or by using the answer as a non-example. Furthermore, teacher can deal with non-academic interruptions through effective use of overlapping with-it-ness.

Listening:
Teachers must avoid teaching tasks that fit their own interests and goals and design activities that address the students' concerns. In order to do this, it is necessary to find out about students and to have a sense of their interests and goals. Teachers can do this by conducting student surveys or simply by questioning and listening to students. Once this information is obtained the teacher can link students' interests with classroom tasks.

Teachers are learning the value of giving assignments that meet the individual abilities and needs of students. After instruction, discussion, questioning, and practice have been provided, rather than assigning one task to all students—teachers are asking students to generate tasks that will show their knowledge of the information presented. Students are given choices and thereby have the opportunity to demonstrate more effectively the skills, concepts, or topics that they as individuals have learned. It has been established that student choice increases student originality, intrinsic motivation, and higher mental processes.

Probing, drawing conclusions, making inferences and summarizing:
The effective teacher uses advanced communication skills such as clarification, probing, drawing conclusions, making inferences, reflection, perception, and summarization as a means to facilitate communication. Teachers who are effective communicators are also good listeners. Teacher behaviors such as eye contact, focusing on student body language, clarifying students' statements, and using "I" messages are effective listeners. The ability to communicate with students, listen effectively, identify relevant and non-relevant information, and summarize students' messages facilitates establishing and maintaining an optimum classroom learning environment.

The value of teacher observations cannot be underestimated. It is through the use of teacher observations that the teacher is able to informally assess the needs of the students during instruction. These observations will drive the lesson and determine the direction that future lessons will take. Teacher observations also set the pace of instruction and ascertain the flow of both student and teacher discourse. After a lesson is carefully planned, teacher observation is the single most important component of an instructional presentation.

One of the primary behaviors that teachers look for in an observation is on-task behavior. There is no doubt that student time on-task directly influences student involvement in instruction and enhances student learning. If the teacher observes that a particular student is not on-task, she will change the method of instruction accordingly. She may change from a teacher-directed approach to a more interactive approach. Questioning will increase in order to cull the participation of the students. If appropriate, the teacher will introduce manipulative materials to the lesson. In addition, teachers may switch to a cooperative group activity thereby removing the responsibility of instruction from the teacher and putting it on the students.

Teachers will also change instructional strategies based on the questions and verbal comments of the students. If the students express confusion, doubt, or are unclear in any way about the content of the lesson, the teacher will immediately take another approach in presenting the lesson. Sometimes this can be accomplished by simply rephrasing an explanation. At other times, it will be necessary for the teacher to use visual organizers or models for understanding to be clear. Effective teachers are sensitive to the reactions and responses of their students and will almost intuitively know when instruction is valid and when it is not. Teachers will constantly check for student comprehension, attention, and focus throughout the presentation of a lesson.

After the teacher has presented a skill or concept lesson she will allow time for the students to practice the skill or concept. At this point it is essential for the teacher to circulate among the students to check for understanding. If the teacher observes that any of the students did not clearly understand the skill or concept, then she must immediately readdress the issue using another technique or approach.

Skill 2.2 Identify ways to correct student errors (e.g., modeling, providing an explanation or additional information, or asking additional questions).

<u>Feedback:</u>
In the old days, students expected teachers would put a letter grade at the top of their papers and perhaps make grammatical corrections to written work. Those days are over. Teachers are now expected to provide feedback to help students learn more.

The amount of time teachers spent grading work yielded little new learning for students. The fear of a low grade alone is not viewed as sufficient to provide students with information as to what was done well and what may need additional work. Students need deeper interaction, particularly as areas of knowledge and skills taught are becoming more complex.

How can a teacher provide appropriate feedback so that students will be able to learn from their assessments? First, language should be helpful and constructive. Critical language does not necessarily help students learn. They may become defensive or hurt, and therefore, they may be more focused on the perceptions than the content. Language that is constructive and helpful will guide students to specific actions and recommendations that would help them improve in the future.

When teachers provide timely feedback, they increase the chance that students will reflect on their thought-processes as they originally produced the work. When feedback comes weeks after the production of an assignment, the student may not remember what it is that caused him or her to respond in a particular way.

Specific feedback is particularly important. Comments like, "This should be clearer" and "Your grammar needs to be worked on" provide information that students may already know. They may already know they have a problem with clarity. Commentary that provides very specific actions students could take to make something more clear or to improve his or her grammar is more beneficial to the student.

Using feedback to promote learning

When teachers provide feedback on a set of assignments, for example, they enhance their students' learning by teaching students how to use the feedback. For example, returning a set of papers can actually do more than provide feedback to students on their initial performance. Teachers can ask students to do additional things to work with their original products, or they can even ask students to take small sections and re-write based on the feedback. While written feedback will enhance student learning, having students do something with the feedback encourages an even deeper learning and reflection.

Experienced teachers may be reading this and thinking, "When will I ever get the time to provide so much feedback?" Although detailed and timely feedback is important—and necessary—teachers do not have to provide it all the time to increase student learning. They can also teach students how to use scoring guides and rubrics to evaluate their own work, particularly before they hand it in to be graded.

One particularly effective way of doing this is by having students examine models and samples of proficient work. Over years, teachers should collect samples, remove names and other identifying factors, and show these examples to students so that they understand what is expected of them. Often, when teachers do this, they will be surprised to see how much students gain from this in terms of their ability to assess their own performance.

Finally, teachers can help students develop plans for revising and improving upon their work, even if it is not evaluated by the teacher in the preliminary stages. For example, teachers can have students keep track of words they commonly misspell, or they can have students make personal lists on areas which they feel they need to focus.

Correctives:

Correctives are defined as the teacher providing an explanation of the error and a correction. For example, the teacher asks the class for a list of verbs. A student answers, "car." The teacher replies, "No, remember, we said a verb shows action. Do you remember what an action is?" The student replies, "Yes, it's doing something." The teacher answers, "Yes, that is correct. Does a car show action?" The student answers, "No." The teacher replies, "No, it doesn't. But what action do we do with a car?" The student answers, "Drive." The teacher responds, "Yes, that is correct. Driving is the action we do with a car, therefore "drive" is a verb. Could you write 'drive' on the board, please."

In this example, the student was led to the correct answer through a series of questions. This technique allows the student to contribute positively to the class, even when he or she is unsure of the answer or has the wrong answer. This leads to more student participation, which directly results in greater subject matter retention.

Redirections:

Redirecting is when the teacher asks a different student to answer the question or to react to the response. For example, a teacher asks, "What is the topic sentence in this paragraph?" A student replies, "Tom had a party." The teacher asks a second student, "Do you agree with that answer?" The second student replies, "Yes." The teacher then has two choices. He or she may either comment on the appropriateness of the answer, or ask the class if anyone disagrees with the first two students.

This technique keeps the students actively involved in the analysis process rather than having them tune out when they had been given the correct answer. This is because, at this point, the students are not sure if the first answer was correct or not. Therefore, they must stay involved until the entire class has reached a consensus.

This type of probing can lead to more student inferences. E. Abraham, M. Nelson and W. Reynolds explained, in a paper presented to the American Educational Research Association in New York in 1971, that they found this to be true. They examined this type of probing in grades one, six and eleven during social studies and math classes. They also discovered that the effects were increased in higher-achieving students, which could be partly due to the teacher.

W. B. Dalton noted in the 1971 study that teachers, in a normal classroom setting, gave more than twice as many positive interactions to their higher-achieving students as they did to their lower-achieving students.

In summary, using correctives and redirects in the classroom leads to greater student involvement. This correlates to higher-level thinking by the students and results in more subject matter retention. The effective teacher is aware of how and when these techniques should be used in the classroom.

Skill 2.3 Identify nonverbal communication strategies that promote student action and performance.

About four to six classroom rules should be posted where students can easily see and read them. These rules should be stated positively, and describe specific behaviors so they are easy to understand. Certain rules may also be tailored to meet target goals and IEP requirements of individual students. (For example, a new student who has had problems with leaving the classroom may need an individual behavior contract to assist him or her with adjusting to the class rule about remaining in the assigned area.) As the students demonstrate the behaviors, the teacher should provide reinforcement and corrective feedback.

Periodic "refresher" practice can be done as needed, for example, after a long holiday or if students begin to "slack off." A copy of the classroom plan should be readily available for substitute use, and the classroom aide should also be familiar with the plan and procedures.

The teacher should clarify and model the expected behavior for the students. In addition to the classroom management plan, a management plan should be developed for special situations, (i.e., fire drills) and transitions (i.e., going to and from the cafeteria). Periodic review of the rules, as well as modeling and practice, may be conducted as needed, such as after an extended school holiday.

Procedures that use social humiliation, withholding of basic needs, pain, or extreme discomfort should never be used in a behavior management plan. Emergency intervention procedures used when the student is a danger to himself or others are not considered behavior management procedures. Throughout the year, the teacher should periodically review the types of interventions being used assess their effectiveness and make revisions as needed.

Success-oriented activities are tasks that are selected to meet the individual needs of the student. During the time a student is learning a new skill, tasks should be selected so that the student will be able to earn a high percentage of correct answers during the teacher questioning and seatwork portions of the lesson. Later, the teacher should also include work that challenges students to apply what they have learned and stimulate their thinking.

Skill knowledge, strategy use, motivation, and personal interests are all factors that influence individual student success. The student who can't be bothered with reading the classroom textbook may be highly motivated to read the driver's handbook for his or her license, or the rulebook for the latest video game. Students who did not master their multiplication tables will likely have problems working with fractions.

In the success-oriented classroom, mistakes are viewed as a natural part of the learning process. The teacher can also show that adults make mistakes by correcting errors without getting unduly upset. The students feel safe to try new things because they know that they have a supportive environment and can correct their mistakes.

Activities that promote student success:
- Are based on useful, relevant content that is clearly specified, and organized for easy learning
- Allow sufficient time to learn the skill and is selected for high rate of success
- Allow students the opportunity to work independently, self-monitor, and set goals

- Provide for frequent monitoring and corrective feedback
- Include collaboration in group activities or peer teaching

Students with learning problems often attribute their successes to luck or ease of the task. Their failures are often blamed on their supposed lack of ability, difficulty of the task, or the fault of someone else. Successful activities, attribution retraining, and learning strategies can help these students to discover that they can become independent learners. When the teacher communicates the expectation that the students can be successful learners and chooses activities that will help them be successful, achievement is increased.

Develop a plan for progression from directed to self-directed activity
Learning progresses in stages from initial acquisition, when the student requires a lot of teacher guidance and instruction, to adaptation, where the student is able to apply what s/he has learned to new situations outside of the classroom. As students progress through the stages of learning, the teacher gradually decreases the amount of direct instruction and guidance. The teacher is slowly encouraging the student to function more independently.

As students progress through the stages of learning, the teacher gradually decreases the amount of direct instruction and guidance and encourages the student to function independently. The ultimate goal of the learning process is to teach students how to be independent and apply their knowledge. A summary of these states and their features appears here:

The ultimate goal of the learning process is to teach students how to become independent and apply their knowledge. A summary of these states and their features appears here:

Stages of Learning Acquisition

State	Teacher Activity	Emphasis
Initial Acquisition	Provide rationale Guidance Demonstration Modeling Shaping Cueing	Errorless learning Backward Chaining (working from the final product backward through the steps) Forward Chaining (proceeding through the steps to a final product)
Advanced Acquisition	Feedback Error correction Specific directions	Criterion evaluation Reinforcement and reward for accuracy
Proficiency	Positive reinforcement Progress monitoring Teach self-management Increased teacher expectations	Increase speed or performance to the automatic level with accuracy Set goals Self-management
Maintenance	Withdraw direct reinforcement Retention and memory Over learning Intermittent schedule of reinforcement	Maintain high level of performance Mnemonic techniques Social and intrinsic reinforcement
Generalization	Corrective feedback	Perform skill in different times and places
Adaptation	Stress independent problem-solving	Independent problem-solving methods No direct guidance or direct instruction

Adapt for transitions

Transition refers to changes in class activities that involve movement. Examples are:

- Breaking up from large group instruction into small groups for learning centers and small-group instructions
- Classroom to lunch, to the playground, or to elective classes
- Finishing reading at the end of one period and getting ready for math the next period
- Emergency situations such as fire drills

Successful transitions are achieved by using proactive strategies. Early in the year, the teacher pinpoints the transition periods in the day and anticipates possible behavior problems, such as students habitually returning late from lunch. After identifying possible problems with the environment or the schedule, the teacher plans proactive strategies to minimize or eliminate those problems.

Proactive planning also gives the teacher the advantage of being prepared, addressing behaviors before they become problems, and incorporating strategies into the classroom management plan right away. Transition plans can be developed for each type of transition and the expected behaviors for each situation taught directly to the students. Some examples might include:

1. Identify the specific behaviors needed for the type of transition.
For example, during a fire drill, students must quickly leave the classroom, walk quietly as a group to the designated exit, proceed to the assigned waiting area, stay with the group, wait for the teacher to receive the all-clear signal, walk quickly and quietly back to the classroom with the group, and re-enter the classroom and return to the seat.

Transition to the cafeteria is similar in the walking procedure, but is different in that cafeteria behavior involves waiting in line for food without cutting, pushing, or bothering others in line, leaving the table area clean and neat, putting trays in the designated area, and perhaps sitting at an assigned table. For each situation, the teacher needs to decide what the student will be expected to do, as well as what possible problems to expect.

2. Develop a set of expectations and teach them to the students.
The expected behaviors should be written in a positive, specific language. Establish a rationale for the rules and provide an explanation of the rules. Provide corrective feedback and reinforcement to the students who demonstrate knowledge of the rules.

3. Model the appropriate behavior.
Guide the students through the procedures and give reinforcement to those who correctly model the behavior.

4. Have the students practice the behaviors independently.
As students practice behaviors, continue corrective feedback and reinforcement. Certain situations, like fire drills, will not be practiced daily, but students will have daily opportunities to demonstrate appropriate transition behavior in and out of class.

NonVerbal Communication:
The Performance Measurement System Domains defines body language as teachers' facial or other body behavior that express interest, excitement, joy, and positive personal relations, or boredom, sadness, dissatisfaction, or negative personal relations, or else, no clear message at all.

The effective teacher communicates non-verbally with students by using positive body language, expressing warmth, concern, acceptance, and enthusiasm. Effective teachers augment their instructional presentations by using positive non-verbal communication such as smiles, open body posture, movement, and eye contact with students. The energy and enthusiasm of the effective teacher can be amplified through positive body language.

Increasing On Task Behavior:
Many factors contribute to student on-task behavior including: student interest in the content, student ability, student attitude, and student needs. Teacher behavior can impact student behavior just as strongly as any other factor. It is imperative that teachers use strategies that encourage and maintain on-task behavior and be aware that they alone may be responsible for motivating students.

A natural way to reinforce on-task behavior is for the teacher to plan activities that reflect children's interests and build lessons based on children's ideas. Teachers guide students through lessons by responding to their questions and ideas, engaging them in conversation, and challenging their thinking.

Once a child-centered foundation has been established for presenting a lesson, the teacher must concentrate on maintaining student focus. To some degree teachers can rely on students' internal motivation to acquire competence. This internal motivation can be greatly affected by the teacher's attitude and enthusiasm. The teacher is a vital role model for promoting student motivation.

Questioning can help maintain focus, direct academic discussions, and create interactive instruction. Questioning can also reinforce content and sustain both on-task behavior and student motivation. Asking questions is a significant part of the instructional process and is most effective when it includes both simple comprehension questions and complex higher order thinking questions.

Skill 2.4 Choose effective communication techniques for conveying high expectations for student learning.

Effective teachers are well versed in the areas of cognitive development, which is crucial to presenting ideas and or materials to students at a level appropriate to their developmental maturity. Effective teachers have the ability to use non-verbal and verbal patterns of communications that focus on age-appropriate instructions and materials.

Consistent with Piagean theory of Cognitive development, younger children (below age eight) have poor language competencies that result in a poor ability to solve complicated problems. Educational instructions and information should be saturated with simplified language to compensate for the limited language competencies of younger children. In contrast, older children (age eight and older) have developed a greater ability to understand language and therefore are capable of solving complex problems. These older children are capable of understanding more advanced instructions and materials that require more advanced language skills.

As the classroom environment increasingly becomes a milieu saturated with cognitive, social, and emotional developmental levels as well as cultural diversity; the teacher must rise to the challenge of presenting ideas and materials appropriate for varying levels of students. Additionally, materials and ideas must be organized, sequenced, and presented to students in a manner consistent with the basic principles of English and in a manner relevant to students as a whole.

Students are likely to achieve at a higher level when they know what they are expected to learn. Besides telling the students what they are going to learn, teachers may choose to use advance organizers that include visual motivations such as outlines, graphs, and models. This practice is especially valuable to the visual learner and is a motivational factor for most students.

Specific questions asked at the beginning of a lesson can also help students focus on the content and be more attentive to instruction. Once the lesson is underway it is further developed by additional questions as well as explanations, checking understanding, making transitions from one topic to another, and sometimes engaging in practice. Teachers who clearly explain difficult points during a lesson and then analyze problems utilizing questioning techniques with the students are more effective than those who do not.

Competency 3.0   Knowledge of strategies for continuous improvement in professional practices for self and school.

Skill 3.1 Identify professional development experiences that will enhance teacher performance and improve student achievement.

Professional development opportunities for teacher performance improvement or enhancement in instructional practices are essential for creating comprehensive learning communities.

In order to promote the vision, mission and action plans of school communities, teachers must be given the toolkits to maximize instructional performances. The development of student-centered learning communities that foster the academic capacities and learning synthesis for all students should be the fundamental goal of professional development for teachers.

The level of professional development may include traditional district workshops that enhance instructional expectations for teachers or the more complicated multiple day workshops given by national and state educational organizations. Most workshops on the national and state level provide clock hours that can be used to renew certifications for teachers every five years. Typically, 150 clock hours is the standard certification number needed to provide a five year certification renewal, so teachers must attend and complete paperwork for a diversity of workshops that range from 1-50 clock hours according to the timeframe of the workshops.

Florida requires districts and schools to provide in-service professional development opportunities for teachers during the school year dealing with district objectives/expectations and relevant workshops or classes that can enhance the teaching practices for teachers. Clock hours are provided with each class or workshop and the type of professional development being offered to teachers determines clock hours. Each year, schools are required to report the number of workshops, along with the participants attending the workshops to the Superintendent's office for filing. Teachers collecting clock hour forms are required to file the forms to maintain certification eligibility and job eligibility.

The research by the National Association of Secondary Principals,' "Breaking Ranks II: Strategies for Leading High School Reform" created the following multiple listing of educational practices needed for expanding the professional development opportunities for teachers:

- Interdisciplinary instruction between subject areas
- Identification of individual learning styles to maximize student academic performance
- Training teachers in understanding and applying multiple assessment formats and implementations in curriculum and instruction
- Looking at multiple methods of classroom management strategies
- Providing teachers with national, federal, state and district curriculum expectations and performance outcomes
- Identifying the school communities' action plan of student learning objectives and teacher instructional practices
- Helping teachers understand how to use data to impact student learning goals and objectives
- Teaching teachers on how to disaggregate student data in improving instruction and curriculum implementation for student academic equity and access
- Develop leadership opportunities for teachers to become school and district trainers to promote effective learning communities for student achievement and success

In promoting professional development opportunities for teachers that enhance student achievement, the bottom line is that teachers must be given the time to complete workshops at no or minimal costs. School and district budgets must include financial resources to support and encourage teachers to engage in mandatory and optional professional development opportunities that create a "win-win" learning experience for students.

Whether a teacher is using criterion-referenced, norm-referenced or performance-based data to inform and impact student learning and achievement, the more important objective is ensuring that teachers know how to effectively use the data to improve and reflect upon existing teaching instructions. The goal of identifying ways for teachers to use the school data is simple, "Is the teacher's instructional practice improving student learning goals and academic success?"

School data can include demographic profiling, cultural and ethic academic trends, state and/or national assessments, portfolios, academic subject pre-post assessment and weekly assessments, projects, and disciplinary reports. By looking at trends and discrepancies in school data, teachers can ascertain whether they are meeting the goals and objectives of the state, national, and federal mandates for school improvement reform and curriculum implementation.

Assessments can be used to motivate students to learn and shape the learning environment to provide learning stimulation that optimizes student access to learning. Butler and McMunn (2006) have shown that "factors that help motivate students to learn are:
1. Involving students in their own assessment,
2. Matching assessment strategies to student learning
3. Consider thinking styles and using assessments to adjust the classroom environment in order to enhance student motivation to learn."

Teachers can shape the way students learn by creating engaging learning opportunities that promote student achievement.

Skill 3.2 Identify ways for using data from learning environments as a basis for exploring and reflecting upon teaching practices.

According to Florida Teacher Certification mandates under code 6A-5.065, the first teacher-accomplished practice for effective teachers is assessment, which is further categorized on three levels; accomplished, professional and pre-professional listed below:

1. **Accomplished Practice One - Assessment**.
   a. Accomplished level. The accomplished teacher uses assessment strategies (traditional and alternate) to assist the continuous development of the learner.
   b. Professional level. The professional teacher continually reviews and assesses data gathered from a variety of sources. These sources can include, but shall not be limited to, pretests, standardized tests, portfolios, anecdotal records, case studies, subject area inventories, cumulative records, and student services information. The professional teacher develops the student's instructional plan that meets cognitive, social, linguistic, cultural, emotional, and physical needs.
   c. Preprofessional level. The preprofessional teacher collects and uses data gathered from a variety of sources. These sources will include both traditional and alternate strategies. Furthermore, the teacher can identify and match the student's instructional plan with their cognitive, social, linguistic, cultural, emotional, and physical needs

(www.floridacertifcationstandards.org).

SEE skill 3.1 also

Competency 004   Knowledge of strategies, materials, and technologies that will promote and enhance critical and creative thinking skills.

Skill 4.1 Identify a variety of instructional strategies, materials, and technologies that foster critical thinking.

Teachers should have built a toolkit of instructional strategies at their disposal. Various materials and technologies should be utilized to encourage problem solving and critical thinking about subject content. Within each curriculum chosen by a district comes an expectation that students must master both benchmarks and standards of various learning skills. There is an established level of academic performance and proficiency in public schools that students are required to master in today's classrooms.

Research of national and state standards indicate that there are additional benchmarks and learning objectives in the subject areas of science, foreign language, English language arts, history, art, health, civics, economics, geography, physical education, mathematics, and social studies that students are required to master in state assessments (Marzano & Kendall, 1996).

A critical thinking skill is a skill target which teachers use to help students develop and sustain learning within specific subject areas and then can be applied to other subject areas. For example, when learning to understand algebraic concepts in solving a math word problem on how much fencing material is needed to build a fence around a backyard area that is 8' x 12', a math student must understand the order of numerical expression in how to simplify algebraic expressions.

Teachers can provide instructional strategies that show students how to group the fencing measurements into an algebraic word problem that with minor addition, subtraction and multiplication can produce a simple number equal to the amount of fencing materials needed to build the fence.

Students use basic skills to understand things that are read, such as a reading passage, a math word problem, or directions for a project. However, students apply additional thinking skills to fully comprehend how what was read could be applied to their own life, how to make comparatives, or what choices could be made based on the factual information given. These higher-order thinking skills are called critical thinking skills as students think about the thinking process, and teachers are instrumental in helping students use these skills in everyday activities.

Examples of these types of skills may include:

- Analyzing bills for overcharges
- Comparing shopping ads or catalogue deals
- Finding the main idea from readings
- Applying what's been learned to new situations
- Gathering information/data from a diversity of sources to plan a project
- Following a sequence of directions
- Looking for cause and effect relationships
- Comparing and contrasting information in synthesizing information

Attention to learner needs during planning is foremost and includes identification of that which the students already know or need to know; the matching of learner needs with instructional elements such as content, materials, activities, and goals; and the determination of whether or not students have performed at an acceptable level, following instruction.

Since most teachers want their educational objectives to include higher level thinking skills, teachers need to direct students toward these higher levels on a taxonomy, such as Bloom's. Questioning is an effective tool to build up students to these higher levels.

Low order questions are useful to begin the process. They insure the student is focused on the required information and understands what needs to be included in the thinking process. For example, if the objective is for students to be able to read and understand the story *Goldilocks and the Three Bears*, the teacher may wish to begin with low order questions (i.e., "What are some things Goldilocks did while in the bears home?" [Knowledge] or "Why didn't Goldilocks like the Papa Bear's chair?" [Analysis]).

Through a series of questions, the teacher can move the students toward the top of the taxonomy. (For example, "If Goldilocks had come to your house, what are some things she may have used?" [Application], "How might the story differed if Goldilocks had visited the three fishes?" [Synthesis], or "Do you think Goldilocks was good or bad? Why?" [Evaluation]). Through questioning, the teacher can control the thinking process of the class. As students become more involved in the discussion they are systematically being lead toward higher levels of thinking.

The ability to create a personal charting of students' academic and emotional growth using performance-based assessment and individualized portfolios becomes a toolkit for both students and teachers. Teachers can use semester portfolios to help gauge student academic progress and personal growth of students. When a student is studying to master a math concept and is able to create visuals of the learning, that transcend beyond the initial concept to create a bridge connecting a higher level of thinking and application of knowledge, then the teacher can share a moment of enjoyable math comprehension with the student.

Using graphic organizers and concept web guides, that center around a concept, and the application of the concept is an instructional strategy teachers can use to guide students into further inquiry of the subject matter. Imagine the research of the German chemist Fredrich August Kekule, when he looked into a fire one night and discovered the molecular structure of benzene. Imagine fostering that same creativity in students and helping students understand the art of visualization and building their creativity of discovery. One of your students may discover the cure for AIDS or cancer or create reading programs for the next generation of readers.

Helping students become effective note-takers and teaching different perspectives for spatial techniques is a proactive teacher strategy in to help create a visual learning environment where art and visualization become natural art forms for learning.

In today's computer environment, students must understand that computers cannot replace the creative thinking and skill application of the human mind.

In the Florida Teacher Certification Standards, code 6A-5.065, critical thinking is the number 4 assessment criteria for effective teacher performance on the three levels below:

1. **Accomplished Practice Four - Critical Thinking.**

    a. <u>Accomplished level.</u> The accomplished teacher uses appropriate techniques and strategies, which promote and enhance critical, creative, and evaluative thinking capabilities of students.
    b. <u>Professional level.</u> The professional teacher will use a variety of performance assessment techniques and strategies that measure higher order thinking skills in students and can provide realistic projects and problem solving activities, which will enable all students to demonstrate their ability to think creatively.
    c. <u>Preprofessional level</u>. The preprofessional teacher is acquiring performance assessment techniques and strategies that measure higher order thinking skills in students and is building a repertoire of realistic projects and problem solving activities designed to assist all students in demonstrating their ability to think creatively.

    (www.floridateachercertificationstandards.org)

Skill 4.2 Identify a variety of instructional strategies, materials, and technologies resources that foster creative thinking.

Teachers who couple diversity in instructional practices with engaging and challenging curriculum and the latest advances in technology can create the ultimate learning environment for creative thinking and continuous learning for students. Teachers who are innovative and creative in instructional practices are able to model and foster creative thinking in their students. Encouraging students to maintain journals or portfolios of their valued work from projects and/or assignments will allow students to make conscious choices on including a diversity of their creative endeavors in a filing format that can be treasured throughout the educational journey.

When teachers are very deliberate about the questions they use with their students, amazing things in the classroom can happen. Most of us remember questions at the end of the chapter in the textbook, or we remember quiz or test questions. While these things potentially have value, they are complete useless if the questions are not crafted well, the purposes for the questions are not defined, and the methods by which students will "answer" the questions are not engaging.

Keep in mind that good questioning does not always imply that there are correct answers (by the way, yes/no questions in the classroom do not provide much in the way of stimulation and thought). Good questioning usually implies that teachers are encouraging deep reflection and active thinking in students. In general, we can say that through questioning, we want students to take risks, solve problems, recall facts, and demonstrate understanding.

When we say that we want students to take risks, we mean that we want them to "try out" various answers and possibilities. By answering a "risk-taking" question, students experiment with their academic voices.

Problem solving questions provoke thought and encourage students to think of questions as entries into problems, not indicators that correct answers are always available in the world.

Even though factual recall questions should not be over-used, it is important to teach students how to comprehend reading, speech, film, or other media. It is also important that students remember certain facts—and questioning can bring on small levels of stress that potentially trigger memory. However, realize that stress may be very upsetting for some students, and such questions, particularly in public settings, may be inappropriate.

Teachers using manipulatives can help students to be able to use their skills in the area of   visual processing. Allowing students to journal can help students understand their own learning. Providing avenues for students to present their understandings to the class using posters and/or Power Point® presentations can be a powerful strategic creative method of teaching and learning.

Finally, by questioning students, we see how much they know. All types of questioning can be done in a variety of formats. For example, we can question students out loud with a whole class. Teachers should refrain from calling on students too often, but occasionally it is an effective technique. Wait time is particularly important: When asking a question, a teacher should not assume that nobody will answer it if a couple seconds have elapsed. Often wait time encourages some students to answer, or it allows all students time to think about the question. Questioning can also take place in small groups or on paper.

Florida Teacher Standard-Code 6A-5.065 Technology

(12) Accomplished Practice Twelve - Technology.
   (a) <u>Accomplished level.</u> The accomplished teacher uses appropriate technology in teaching and learning processes.
   (b) <u>Professional level.</u> The professional teacher uses technology (as appropriate) to establish an atmosphere of active learning with existing and emerging technologies available at the school site. She/he provides students with opportunities to use technology to gather and share information with others, and facilitates access to the use of electronic resources.
   (c) <u>Preprofessional level.</u> The preprofessional teacher uses technology as available at the school site and as appropriate to the learner. She/he provides students with opportunities to actively use technology and facilitates access to the use of electronic resources. The teacher also uses technology to manage, evaluate, and improve instruction.

Competency 5.0 **Knowledge of cultural, linguistic, and learning style differences and how these differences affect classroom practice and student learning.**

Skill 5.1 Identify instructional and interpersonal skills and classroom practices that encourage innovation and create a positive learning climate for all students.

A positive self-concept for a child or adolescent is a very important element. In terms of the students' ability to learn and to be an integral member of society self concept and interpersonal skills provide the foundation upon which all learning is based. If students think poorly of themselves or have sustained feelings of inferiority, they may not be able to optimize their potential for learning. It is therefore part of the teacher's task to ensure that each student develops a positive self-concept.

A positive self-concept does not imply feelings of superiority, perfection, or competence/efficacy. Instead, a positive self-concept involves self-acceptance as a person, liking himself/herself, and having a proper respect for oneself. The teacher who encourages these factors has contributed to the development of a positive self-concept in students.

Teachers can take a number of different approaches to enhance the self-concept of students. One such scheme is called the process approach, which proposes a three-phase model for teaching. This model includes a sensing function, a transforming function, and an acting function. These three factors can be simplified into the words by which the model is usually given: reach, touch, and teach. The sensing, or perceptual, function incorporates information or stimuli in an intuitive manner. The transforming function conceptualizes abstracts, evaluates, and provides meaning and value to perceived information. The acting function chooses actions from several different alternatives to be set forth overtly. The process model may be applied to almost any curricular field.

An approach that aims directly at the enhancement of self concept is designated as Invitational Education. According to this approach, teachers and their behaviors may be inviting or they may be disinviting. Inviting behaviors enhance self-concept among students, while disinviting behaviors diminish self-concept.

Disinviting behaviors include those that demean students, as well as those that may be chauvinistic, sexist, condescending, thoughtless, or insensitive to student feelings. Inviting behaviors are the opposite of these, and characterize teachers who act with consistency and sensitivity. Inviting teacher behaviors reflect an attitude of *doing with* rather than *doing to."* Students are invited or disinvited depending on the teacher behaviors.

Invitational teachers exhibit the following skills (Biehler and Snowman, 394):

- Reaching each student (e.g., learning names, having one-to-one contact)
- Listening with care (e.g., picking up subtle cues)
- Being real with students (e.g., providing only realistic praise, "coming on straight")
- Being real with oneself (e.g., honestly appraising your own feelings and disappointments)
- Inviting good discipline (e.g., showing students you have respect in personal ways)
- Handling rejection (e.g., not taking lack of student response in personal ways)
- Inviting oneself (e.g., thinking positively about oneself)

Cooperative Learning:
Cooperative learning situations, as practiced in today's classrooms, grew out of research conducted by several groups in the early 1970's. Cooperative learning situations can range from very formal applications such as STAD (Student Teams-Achievement Divisions) and CIRC (Cooperative Integrated Reading and Composition) to less formal groupings known variously as *group investigation*, *learning together*, or *discovery groups*. Cooperative learning as a general term is now firmly recognized and established as a teaching and learning technique in American schools.

Since cooperative learning techniques are so widely diffused in the schools, it is necessary to orient students in the skills by which cooperative learning groups can operate smoothly. Students who cannot interact constructively with other students will not be able to take advantage of the learning opportunities provided by the cooperative learning situations and will furthermore deprive their fellow students of the opportunity for cooperative learning.

These skills form the hierarchy of cooperation in which students' first learn to work together as a group, so they may then proceed to levels at which they may engage in simulated conflict situations. This cooperative setting allows different points of view to be constructively entertained.

Skill 5.2 Select materials and strategies that encourage learning about diverse cultural groups.

Effective teaching and learning for students begins with teachers who can demonstrate sensitivity for diversity in teaching and relationships within school communities. Student portfolios should include work that includes a multicultural perspective. Teachers also need to be responsive to including cultural and diverse resources in their curriculum and instructional practices.

Exposing students to culturally sensitive room decorations or posters that show positive and inclusive messages is one way to demonstrate inclusion of multiple cultures. Teachers should also continuously make cultural connections that are relevant and empowering for all students while communicating academic and behavioral expectations. Cultural sensitivity is communicated beyond the classroom with parents and community members to establish and maintain relationships.

Diversity can be further defined as the following:
- Differences among learners, classroom settings and academic outcomes
- Biological, sociological, ethnicity, socioeconomic status psychological needs, learning modalities and styles among learners
- Differences in classroom settings that promote learning opportunities such as collaborative, participatory, and individualized learning groupings
- Expected learning outcomes that are theoretical, affective and cognitive for students

Teachers should establish a classroom climate that is culturally respectful and engaging for students. In a culturally sensitive classroom, teachers maintain equity and fairness in student interactions and curriculum implementation. Assessments include cultural responses and perspectives that become further learning opportunities for students. Other artifacts that could reflect teacher/student sensitivity to diversity might consist of the following:

- Student portfolios reflecting multicultural/multiethnic perspectives
- Journals and reflections from field trips/ guest speakers from diverse cultural backgrounds
- Printed materials and wall displays from multicultural perspectives
- Parent/guardian letters in a variety of languages reflecting cultural diversity
- Projects that include cultural history and diverse inclusions
- Disaggregated student data reflecting cultural groups
- Classroom climate of professionalism that fosters diversity and cultural inclusion

The encouragement of diversity education allows teachers a variety of opportunities to expand their experiences with students, staff, community members and parents from culturally diverse backgrounds.   These experiences can be proactively applied to promote cultural diversity inclusion in the classroom. Teachers are able to engage and challenge students to develop and incorporate their own diversity skills in building character and relationships with cultures beyond their own. In changing the thinking patterns of students to become more cultural inclusive in the 21st century, teachers are addressing the globalization of our world.

The Florida Teacher Standard Code 6A-5.065 shown below further exemplifies the importance of diversity in the classroom.

Florida Teacher Standard-Code 6A-5.065 Diversity
(5) **Accomplished Practice Five - Diversity.**
  (a) Accomplished level. The accomplished teacher uses teaching and learning strategies that reflect each student's culture, learning styles, special needs, and socio-economic background.
  (b) Professional level. The professional teacher establishes a risk-taking environment, which accepts and fosters diversity. The teacher must demonstrate knowledge of varied cultures by practices such as conflict resolution, mediation, creating a climate of openness, inquiry and support.
  (c) Preprofessional level. The preprofessional teacher establishes a comfortable environment, which accepts and fosters diversity. The teacher must demonstrate knowledge and awareness of varied cultures. The teacher creates a climate of openness, inquiry, and support by practicing strategies as acceptance, tolerance, resolution, and mediation.

Competency 6.0 **Knowledge of the Code of Ethics and Principles of Professional Conduct of the Education Profession in Florida.**

Skill 6.1 Apply the Code of Ethics and Principles of Professional Conduct to realistic professional and personal situations.

Florida Code of Ethics-Education Profession 6B-1.001

The Florida Code of Ethics for teachers is extensive in both its professional and personal expectations for teachers within the classroom. All codes are taken directly from the state code of ethics and applied to realistic personal and professional situations in the classroom.

> **(1) The educator values the worth and dignity of every person, the pursuit of truth, devotion to excellence, acquisition of knowledge, and the nurture of democratic citizenship. Essential to the achievement of these standards are the freedoms to learn and to teach and the guarantee of equal opportunity for all.**

The ultimate goal of teachers when they enter the profession of teaching is to provide a comprehensive education for all students by providing challenging curriculum and setting high expectations for learning. In an ideal classroom, the mechanisms for providing the perfect teaching climate and instruction are the norm and not the exception. Given the diversity of learners, the reality is that teachers are confronted with classrooms that are infused with management issues and a significant variety of differentiated learning needs.

Researchers have shown that for new teachers entering the profession, the two greatest obstacles are dealing with increasing behavioral issues in the classroom and dealing with students who are minimally engaged in their own learning process. The goal of teachers is to maintain a toolkit of resources to be able to deal with the ever-changing landscape of learners and classroom environments.

> **(2) The educator's primary professional concern will always be for the student and for the development of the student's potential. The educator will therefore strive for professional growth and will seek to exercise the best professional judgment and integrity.**

In a student-centered learning environment, the goal is to provide the best opportunity for academic success for all students. Integrating the developmental patterns of physical, social and academic norms for students will provide individual learners with student learning plans that are individualized and specific to their skill levels and needs.

Teachers who effectively develop and maximize a student's potential will use pre- and post-assessments to gather comprehensive data on the existing skill level of the student and then plan and adapt the curriculum to address student skills. Maintaining communication with the student and parents will provide a community approach to learning where all stakeholders are included to maximize student-learning growth.

> **(3) Aware of the importance of maintaining the respect and confidence of one's colleagues, of students, of parents, and of other members of the community, the educator strives to achieve and sustain the highest degree of ethical conduct.**

The ethical conduct of an educator has undergone extensive scrutiny in today's classrooms. Teachers are under intense rules and regulations to maintain the highest degree of conduct and professionalism in the classroom. Current court cases in Florida have examined ethical violations of teachers engaged in improper communication and abuse with students, along with teachers engaged in drug violations and substance abuse in classrooms. It is imperative that teachers educating today's young people have the highest regard for professionalism and be proper role models for students in and out of the classrooms.

Skill 6.2 Identify statutory grounds and procedures for disciplinary action, the penalties that can be imposed by the Educational Practices Commission against a certificate holder, and the appeals process available to the individual.

The Florida Code of Professional Conduct for Teachers contains a number of obligatory expectations that are intended to protect both the teacher and the student. The penalties for educators who violate the professional codes could result in permanent revocation or suspension of their certification. The listing below shows the conditions of employment for teachers.

It is important teachers understand and take seriously their professional roles as certified employees with the state of Florida. Creating a safe learning environment and protecting students from any conditions that could be potentially harmful or cause degradation is the first obligation teachers have to students. Being a role model who exemplifies good character and ethical professionalism are the next principles teachers must maintain in order to avoid potential disciplinary action or certificate revocation.

6B-1.006 Principles of Professional Conduct for the Education Profession in Florida.

(1) The following disciplinary rule shall constitute the Principles of Professional Conduct for the Education Profession in Florida.

(2) Violation of any of these principles shall subject the individual to revocation or suspension of the individual educator's certificate, or the other penalties as provided by law.

(3) Obligation to the student requires that the individual:

- Shall make reasonable effort to protect the student from conditions
- Shall make reasonable efforts to protect the student from conditions harmful to learning and/or to the student's mental and/or physical health and/or safety.
- Shall not withhold information regarding a position from an applicant or misrepresent an assignment or conditions of employment.
- Shall provide upon the request of the certificated individual a written statement of specific reason for recommendations that lead to the denial of increments, significant changes in employment, or termination of employment.
- Shall not assist entry into or continuance in the profession of any person known to be unqualified in accordance with these Principles of Professional Conduct for the Education Profession in Florida and other applicable Florida Statutes and State Board of Education Rules.
- Shall self-report within forty-eight (48) hours to appropriate authorities (as determined by district) any arrests/charges involving the abuse of a child or the sale and/or possession of a controlled substance. Such notice shall not be considered an admission of guilt nor shall such notice be admissible for any purpose in any proceeding, civil or criminal, administrative or judicial, investigatory or adjudicatory. In addition, shall self-report any conviction, finding of guilt, withholding of adjudication, commitment to a pretrial diversion program, or entering of a plea of guilty or Nolo Contendre for any criminal offense other than a minor traffic violation within forty-eight (48) hours after the final judgment. When handling sealed and expunged records disclosed under this rule, school districts shall comply with the confidentiality provisions of Sections 943.0585(4)(c) and 943.059(4)(c), Florida Statutes.
- Shall report to appropriate authorities any known allegation of a violation of the Florida School Code or State Board of Education Rules as defined in Section 1012.795(1), Florida Statutes.

(www.floridacodeofconductteachers.org)

Self-reporting issues of abuse or criminal activity within forty eight hours is mandatory for teachers involved in any arrests/charges involving the abuse of a child or the sale or possession of illegal drugs. Teachers are put on immediate suspension with pay pending the outcome of an investigation. District investigators are sent to school communities to gather data from witnesses, computers, and administrators to provide evidence to either support or refute the pending case.

Teachers can appeal a suspension by sending a letter to the district either personally or from a lawyer representative to appeal the suspension and refute the charges. The School Board makes the final decision to revoke or suspend a certificate if the charges are not criminally pending by the police or through the legal system. The Superintendent provides the final closure on the filing of revoked or suspended certificates.

Competency 7.0 **Knowledge of how to apply human development and learning theories that support the intellectual, personal, and social development of all students.**

Skill 7.1 Identify patterns of physical, social, and academic development of students.

The teacher needs a broad knowledge and thorough understanding of the development that typically occurs during the students' current period of life. More importantly, the teacher needs to understand how children learn best during each period of development. The most important premise of child development is that all domains of development (physical, social, and academic) are integrated. Development in each dimension is influenced by the other dimensions. Moreover, today's educator must also have a knowledge of disabilities and how these disabilities effect all domains of a child's development.

Physical Development
It is important for the teacher to be aware of the physical stage of development and how the child's physical growth and development affect the child's learning. Factors determined by the physical stage of development include: ability to sit and attend, the need for activity, the relationship between physical skills and self-esteem, and the degree to which physical involvement in an activity (as opposed to being able to understand an abstract concept) affects learning.

Cognitive (Academic) Development
Children progress through patterns of learning beginning with pre-operational thought processes and moving to concrete operational thoughts. Eventually they begin to acquire the mental ability to think about and solve problems in their head because they can manipulate objects symbolically. Children of most ages can use symbols such as words and numbers to represent objects and relations, but they need concrete reference points. It is essential children be encouraged to use and develop the thinking skills that they possess in solving problems that are of interest to them. The content of the curriculum must be relevant, engaging, and meaningful to the students.

Social Development

Children progress through a variety of social stages beginning with an awareness of peers but a lack of concern for the presence of these peers. Young children engage in "parallel" activities (playing alongside their peers without directly interacting with one another.) During the primary years, children develop an intense interest in peers.

They establish productive, positive, social, and working relationships with one another. This stage of social growth continues to increase in importance throughout the child's school years . It is necessary for the teacher to recognize the importance of developing positive peer group relationships and to provide opportunities and support for cooperative small group projects which not only develop cognitive ability but promote peer interaction. The ability to work and relate effectively with peers is of major importance and contributes greatly to the child's sense of competence. In order to develop this sense of competence, children need to be successful in acquiring the knowledge and skills recognized by our culture as important, especially those skills which promote academic achievement.

Knowledge of age-appropriate expectations is fundamental to the teacher's positive relationship with students and effective instructional strategies. Equally important is the knowledge of what is individually appropriate for the specific children in a classroom. Developmentally oriented teachers approach classroom groups and individual students with a respect for their emerging capabilities. Developmentalists recognize that students progress through common patterns, but at different rates which usually cannot be accelerated by adult pressure or input.

Developmentally oriented teachers understand that variance in the school performance of different children often results from differences in their general growth. With the establishment of inclusionary classes throughout the schools, it is vital for all teachers to know the characteristics of students' exceptionalities and their implications on learning.

Skill 7.2 Identify motivational strategies and factors that encourage students to be achievement and goal oriented.

Teachers need to be aware that much of what they say and do can be motivating and may have a positive effect on students' achievement. Studies have been conducted to determine the impact of teacher behavior on student performance. Surprisingly, a teacher's voice can really make an impression on students. Teachers' voices have several dimensions—volume, pitch, rate, etc. A recent study on the effects of speech rate indicates that, although both boys and girls prefer to listen at the rate of about 200 words per minute, boys tend to prefer slower rates overall than girls. This same study indicates that a slower rate of speech directly affects processing ability and comprehension.

Other speech factors such as communication of ideas, communication of emotion, distinctness/pronunciation, quality variation and phrasing, correlate with teaching criterion scores. These scores show that "good" teachers ("good" meaning teachers who positively impact and motivate students) use more variety in speech than do "less effective" teachers. A teacher's speech skills can be strong motivating elements. A teacher's body language has an even greater effect on student achievement and ability to set and focus on goals.

Teacher smiles provide support and give feedback about the teacher's affective state. A deadpan expression can actually be a detriment to the student's progress. Teacher frowns are perceived by students to mean displeasure, disapproval, and even anger. Studies also show that teacher posture and movement are indicators of the teacher's enthusiasm and energy, which emphatically influence student learning, attitudes, motivation, and focus on goals. Teachers have a greater efficacy on student motivation than any person other than parents.

Teachers can also enhance student motivation by planning and directing interactive, hands-on learning experiences. Research substantiates that cooperative group projects decrease student behavior problems and increase student on-task behavior. Students who are directly involved with learning activities are more motivated to complete a task to the best of their ability.

Skill 7.3 Identify activities to accommodate different learning needs, developmental levels, and experiential backgrounds.

The effective teacher is cognizant of students' individual learning styles as well as human growth and development theory. S/he then applies these principles to the selection and implementation of appropriate classroom instructional activities.

Learning activities selected for younger students (below age eight) should focus on short time frames and be in a highly simplified form. The nature of the activity and the content in which the activity is presented affects the approach the students will use to process the information. Younger children tend to process information at a slower pace than children aged eight and older.

On the other hand, when selecting and implementing learning activities for older children, teachers should focus on more complex ideas. Older students are capable of understanding more complex instructional activities. Moreover, effective teachers maintain a clear understanding of the developmental appropriateness of activities selected.

The effective teacher takes care to select appropriate activities and classroom situations in which learning is optimized. The classroom teacher should manipulate instructional activities and classroom conditions in a manner that enhances group and individual learning opportunities. For example, the classroom teacher can organize group learning activities in which students are placed in a situation in which cooperation, sharing ideas, and discussion occurs. Cooperative learning activities can assist students in learning to collaborate share personal and cultural ideas and values in a classroom learning environment.

The effective teacher plans his/her learning activities as to introduce them in a meaningful instructional sequence. Teachers should combine instructional activities as to reinforce information by providing students with relevant learning experiences throughout instructional activities.

The effective teacher selects learning activities based on specific learning objectives. Ideally, teachers should not plan activities that fail to augment the specific objectives of the lesson. Learning activities should be planned with a learning objective in mind. Objective driven learning activities tend to serve as a tool to reinforce the teacher's lesson presentation. Additionally, teacher selected learning objectives should be aligned with state and district educational goals. State and district goals should focus on National Educational Goals (Goals 2000) and the specific strengths and weaknesses of individual students assigned to their class.

Skill 7.4 Apply knowledge of learning theories to classroom practices.

There are many factors that affect student learning including: how students learn, how learning is presented, amount of background knowledge and/or experiences. There are several educational learning theories which can be applied to classroom practices. One classic learning theory is Piaget's stages of development which consist of four learning stages:
- Sensory motor stage (from birth to age 2)
- Pre-operation stages (ages 2 to 7 or early elementary)
- Concrete operational (ages7 to 11 or upper elementary)
- Formal operational (ages 7-15 or late elementary/high school).

Piaget believed children passed through this series of stages as they developed from the most basic forms of concrete thinking to the most sophisticated levels of abstract thinking.

Two of the most prominent learning theories in education today are Brain-Based Learning and the Multiple Intelligence Theory. Recent brain research suggests that increased knowledge about the way the brain retains information will enable educators to design the most effective learning environments. As a result, researchers have developed twelve principles that relate knowledge about the brain to teaching practices. These twelve principles of Brain-based Learning Theory are:

- The brain is a complex adaptive system
- The brain is social
- The search for meaning is innate
- We use patterns to learn more effectively
- Emotions are crucial to developing patterns
- Each brain perceives and creates parts and whole simultaneously
- Learning involves focused and peripheral attention
- Learning involves conscious and unconscious processes
- We have at least two ways of organizing memory
- Learning is developmental
- Complex learning is enhanced by challenged (and inhibited by threat)
- Every brain is unique
  (Caine & Caine, 1994, Mind/Brain Learning Principles)

Educators can use these principles to help design methods and environments in their classrooms to maximize student learning.

The Multiple Intelligent Theory, developed by Howard Gardner, suggests that students learn in (at least) seven different ways. These include: visually/spatially, musically, verbally, logically/mathematically, interpersonally, intrapersonally, and bodily/kinesthetically.

Another learning theory is that of Constructivism. The theory of constructivist learning allows students to construct learning opportunities. For constructivist teachers, the belief is that students create their own reality of knowledge and how to process and observe the world around them. Students are constantly constructing new ideas, which serve as frameworks for learning and teaching. Researchers have shown that the constructivist model is comprised of the following four components:

- Learner creates knowledge
- Learner constructs and makes meaningful new knowledge to existing knowledge
- Learner shapes and constructs knowledge by life experiences and social interactions

In constructivist learning communities, the student, teacher and classmates establish knowledge cooperatively on a daily basis

Kelly (1969) states "human beings construct knowledge systems based on their observations parallels Piaget's theory that individuals construct knowledge systems as they work with others who share a common background of thought and processes." Constructivist learning for students is dynamic and ongoing. For constructivist teachers, the classroom becomes a place where students are encouraged to interact with the instructional process by asking questions and posing new ideas to old theories. The use of cooperative learning which encourages students to work in supportive learning environments using their own ideas to stimulate questions and propose outcomes is a major aspect of a constructivist classroom.

Yet another learning theory is that of metacognition. The metacognition learning theory deals with "the study of how to help the learner gain understanding about how knowledge is constructed and about the conscious tools for constructing that knowledge" (Joyce and Weil 1996). The metacognitive approach to learning involves the teacher's understanding that teaching the student to process his/her own learning and mastery of skill provides the greatest learning and retention opportunities in the classroom. Students are taught to develop concepts and teach themselves skills in problem solving and critical thinking. The student becomes an active participant in the learning process and the teacher facilitates that conceptual and cognitive learning process.

Finally, social and behavioral theories look at the social interactions of students in the classroom that instruct or impact learning opportunities in the classroom. The psychological approaches behind both theories are subject to individual variables that are learned and applied either proactively or negatively in the classroom. The stimulus of the classroom can promote conducive learning or evoke behavior that is counterproductive for both students and teachers. Students are social beings that normally gravitate to action in the classroom, so teachers must be cognizant in planning classroom environments that provide both focus and engagement in maximizing learning opportunities.

Skill 7.5 Identify characteristics of and intervention strategies for, students with disabilities.

There are many types of disabilities found in children and adults. Some disabilities are entirely physical, while others are entirely related to learning and the mind. Some involve a combination of both. When teacher's notice abnormalities in the classroom, such as a student's incredible ability to solve a math problem without working it out (a potential attribute of giftedness) or another student's extreme trouble with spelling (a potential attribute of dyslexia), a teacher may suspect a disability is present.

Common learning disabilities include:
- Attention deficit hyperactivity disorder (where concentration can be very difficult)
- Auditory processing disorders (where listening comprehension is very difficult)
- Visual processing disorders (where reading and/or visual memory may be impaired),
- Dyslexia (where reading may be difficult)

Some physical disabilities include:
- Down's Syndrome
- Cerebral Palsy

Developmental disabilities might include the lack of ability to use fine motor skills.

When giftedness is observed, teachers should also concern themselves with ensuring that such children receive the attention they need and deserve so they can continue to learn and grow.

The list of possible disabilities is almost endless. When noticed, teachers might seek the help of specialists within their school to determine if further testing or intervention is needed.

A teacher's responsibility to students extends beyond the four walls of the school building. In addition to offering well-planned and articulately delivered lessons, the teacher must consider the effects of both body language and spoken language on students' learning. Furthermore, today's educator must address the needs of diverse learners within a single classroom. The teacher is able to attain materials that may be necessary for the majority of the regular education students and some of the special needs children and, more and more frequently, one individual student. The effective teacher knows that there are currently hundreds of adaptive materials that could be used to help these students increase achievement and develop skills.

Student-centered classrooms contain not only textbooks, workbooks, and literature materials but also rely heavily on a variety of audio-visual equipment and computers. There are tape recorders, language masters, filmstrip projectors, and laser disc players to help meet the learning styles of some of the students.

Although most school centers cannot supply all of the possible materials all special needs students within their school may require, each district, more than likely, has a resource center where teachers can borrow special equipment. Most community support agencies offer assistance in providing necessary equipment or materials to serve students and adults with special needs. Teachers must be familiar with procedures to obtain a wide range of materials including school supplies, medical care, clothing, food, adaptive computers, books (such as Braille), eye glasses, hearing aids, wheelchairs, counseling, transportation, and many others.

A teacher's job would be relatively easy if simply instructing students in current curriculum objectives was his/her only responsibility. Today's educator must first assure that the students are able to come to school, are able to attend to the curriculum, have individual learning styles met, and are motivated to work to their fullest capacity.

Many special needs students have an Individual Educational Plan (IEP) or a 504 Plan. These documents clearly state the students' educational objectives and learning needs, as well as persons responsible for meeting these objectives.

A well-written Individual Educational Plan will contain evidence that the student is receiving resources from the school and the community that will assist in helping to meet the physical, social and academic needs of the student.

The challenges of meeting the needs of all students in the classroom require that the teacher himself be a lifelong learner. Ongoing participation in professional staff development, attendance at local, state, and national conferences, and continuing education classes help teachers grow in many ways including an awareness of resources available for students.

Individuals with Disabilities Act and Child Study Teams

Collaborative teams play a crucial role in meeting the needs of all students, and they are an important step in helping to identify students with special needs. Under the Individuals with Disabilities Act (IDEA), which federally mandates special education services in every state, it is the responsibility of public schools to ensure consultative, evaluative and, if necessary, prescriptive services to children with special needs.

In most school districts, this responsibility is handled by a collaborative group of professionals called the Child Study Team (CST). If a teacher or parent suspects a child is experiencing academic, social or emotional problems a referral can be made to the CST. The CST is a team consisting of educational professionals (including teachers, specialists, the school psychologist, guidance, and other support staff) who will review the student's case and situation through meetings with the teacher and/or parents/guardians. The CST will determine what evaluations or tests are necessary, if any, and will also discuss the results. Based on these results, the CST will suggest a plan of action if one is necessary.

Inclusion, mainstreaming, and least restrictive environment
Inclusion, mainstreaming and least restrictive environment are interrelated policies under the IDEA, with varying degrees of statutory imperatives.
- Inclusion is the right of students with disabilities to be placed in the regular classroom
- Lease restrictive environment is the mandate that children be educated to the maximum extent appropriate with their non-disabled peers *excluded*
- Mainstreaming is a policy where disabled students can be placed in the regular classroom, as long as such placement does not interfere with the student's educational plan

One plan of action is an Academic Intervention Plan (AIP). An AIP consists of additional instructional services that are provided to the student in order to help them better achieve academically. Often these plans are developed if the student has met certain criteria (such as scoring below the state reference point on standardized tests or performing more than two levels below grade-level).

Another plan of action is a 504 plan. A 504 plan is a legal document based on the provisions of the Rehabilitation Act of 1973 (which preceded IDEA). A 504 plan is a plan of instructional services to assist students with special needs in a regular education classroom setting. When a student's physical, emotional, or other impairments (such as Attention Deficit Disorder) impact his or her ability to learn in a regular education classroom setting, that student can be referred for a 504 meeting. Typically, the CST and perhaps even the student's physician or therapist will participate in the 504 meeting and review the student's specific needs to determine if a 504 plan will be written.

Finally, a child referred to CST may qualify for an Individualized Education Plan (IEP). An IEP is a legal document which delineates the specific, adapted services a student with disabilities will receive. An IEP differs from a 504 plan in that the child must be identified for special education services to qualify for an IEP, and all students who receive special education services must have an IEP. Each IEP must contain statements pertaining to the student's present performance level, annual goals, related services and supplementary aids, testing modifications, a projected date of services, and assessment methods for monitoring progress. At least once each year, the CST and guardians must meet to review and update a student's IEP.

Special education teachers, resource specialists, school psychologists, and other special education staff are present on school campuses to be resources for students who have special educational needs. Occasionally, new teachers fear that when a resource specialist seeks to work with them, it means that the resource specialist does not think they are doing an adequate job in dealing with students with Individualized Education Plans (IEPs). Quite the contrary is true. Many IEPs require that resource specialists work in students' general education classrooms. Considering that school is more than just about the learning of content standards—that it is often about socialization and the development of citizens for a democratic society—it is both counterproductive and unfair to exclude students from regular classrooms, even if they need some individualized assistance from a special education resource teacher.

First and foremost, teachers must be familiar with what is stated in their students' IEPs. For example, some IEPs have explicit strategies that teachers should use to help the students learn effectively. Additionally, teachers may want to provide additional attention to these students to ensure that they are progressing effectively. Sometimes, it may be necessary to reduce or modify assignments for students with disabilities. For example, if a teacher were to assign fifteen math problems for homework, for particular students, the assignment might be more effective if it is five problems for the students with disabilities. Teachers can use multiple strategies, group students in flexible situations, and pair them with others who can be of greater assistance.

Finally, welcome and include the suggestions and assistance of the special education staff. Most resource specialists are trained particularly to work with general education teachers, and most want to be able to do that in the most effective, non-threatening way.

Special education services are offered in many ways, and a student's IEP will determine their least restrictive environment. Inclusion refers to the situation where a student with special needs remains in the regular education classroom with the support of special education support staff (sometimes in the form of a personal or class aid). Sometimes, a student requires some resource room, or pull out, services. In these cases, students are taken into smaller class settings where personalized services are delivered in their greatest area(s) of difficulty. Students who have difficulty functioning in a regular education classroom are placed in smaller classrooms for the full school day. These are sometimes referred to as LD, or learning disabled, classrooms.

Per federal law, students with disabilities should be included as much as possible in the general education curriculum of their schools. While this may be difficult for new teachers (likewise, it may be difficult for new teachers to include gifted students in the general education curriculum), it is extremely important to do so.

Flexible grouping is a unique strategy to ensure that students with special needs are fully accommodated. While flexible grouping can indeed involve groups for various learning activities that will change (depending on the activity, or just depending on the need to rotate groups), when teachers consistently build in various group structures in order to accommodate various learning needs, their students will get varied and multiple opportunities to talk about, reflect upon, and question new learning. In some cases, teachers may wish to pair students with special needs with other students who are proficient in particular subjects; at other times, they may desire to pair students with others who have similar levels of proficiency.

Behavior issues often cause students with special needs to be excluded from full class participation. It is important for teachers to note that often, students with special needs do not want to be excluded, and often, they do not want to be "bad. " Rather, they are seeking attention, or they are bored. In either case, classroom activities must be developed with these concerns in mind. All students, in fact, will be more engaged with hands-on, real-world learning activities. Often, when teachers give students even small amounts of choice, such as letting them choose one of three topics to write about, students feel empowered. Students with special needs are no different.

Finally, many students with special needs want to stay "caught up" with the rest of the class, but occasionally, they cannot. In such cases, it is imperative that teachers find ways that will allow these students to know that they are on the same page as the rest of the class. Reducing the amount of work for students with special needs is often productive; pairing such students with more proficient students can also be assistive.

Students with exceptional abilities can be a great challenge for teachers. It is very unfair to assume that since these students already "get it" that they can be ignored. These students need to continue to learn, even if it is above and beyond the rest of the class. Furthermore, they will often resent being so much smarter than the rest of the class because they are "called on" more or they are treated as if they do not need any attention. First, while these students are a fantastic resource for the rest of the class, being a resource is not their role in the classroom. They are there to learn, just like the rest of the class. They occasionally need different work to engage them and stimulate their minds. They do not simply need more work; this is unfair to them, and it is insulting.

Competency 8.0   Knowledge of effective reading strategies that can be applied across the curriculum to increase learning.

Skill 8.1   Identify effective instructional methods to develop text reading skills (i.e., phonemic awareness, phonics, and fluency).

In 2000, the National Reading Panel released its now well-known report on teaching children to read. In a way, this report slightly put to rest the debate between phonics and whole-language. It argued, essentially, that word-letter recognition was as important as was understanding of what the text means. The report's "Big 5" critical areas of reading instruction are as follows:

Phonemic Awareness

The acknowledgement of sounds and words, for example, a child's realization that some words rhyme is one of the skills that fall under this category. Onset and rhyme are skills that might help students learn that the sound of the first letter "b" in the word "bad" can be changed with the sound "d" to make it "dad." The key in phonemic awareness is that when you teach it to children, it can be taught with the students' eyes closed. In other words, it's all about sounds, not about ascribing written letters to sounds.

Phonics

As opposed to phonemic awareness, the study of phonics must be done with the eyes open. It's the connection between the sounds and letters on a page. In other words, students learning phonics might see the word "bad" and sound each letter out slowly until they recognize that they just said the word.

Fluency

When students practice fluency, they practice reading connected pieces of text. In other words, instead of looking at a word as just a word, they might read a sentence straight through. The point of fluency is for the student to comprehend what she is reading. She would need to be able to "fluently" piece words in a sentence together quickly. If a student is NOT fluent in reading, he or she would sound each letter or word out slowly and pay more attention to the phonics of each word. A fluent reader, on the other hand, might read a sentence out loud using appropriate intonations.

The best way to test for fluency is to have a student read something out loud, preferably a few sentences in a row—or more. Sure, most students just learning to read will probably not be very fluent right away; but with practice, they will increase their fluency. Even though fluency is not the same as comprehension, it is said that fluency is a good predictor of comprehension. Think about it: If you're focusing too much on sounding out each word, you're not going to be paying attention to the meaning.

Comprehension

Comprehension simply means that the reader can ascribe meaning to text. Even though students may be good with phonics, and even know what many words on a page mean, some of them are not able to demonstrate comprehension because they do not have the strategies that would help them to comprehend. For example, students should know that stories often have structures (beginning, middle, and end). They should also know that when they are reading something and it does not make sense, they will need to employ "fix-up" strategies where they go back into the text they just read and look for clues. Teachers can use many strategies to teach comprehension, including questioning, asking students to paraphrase or summarize, utilizing graphic organizers, and focusing on mental images.

Vocabulary

Students will be better at comprehension if they have a stronger working vocabulary. Research has shown that students learn more vocabulary when it is presented in context, rather than in vocabulary lists, for example. Furthermore, the more students get to use particular words in context, the more they will (a) remember each word, and (b) utilize it in the comprehension of sentences that contain the words.

Methods used to teach these skills are often featured in a *balanced literacy* curriculum which focuses on the use of skills in various instructional contexts. For example, with independent reading, students independently choose books that are at their reading levels; with guided reading, teachers work with small groups of students to help them with their particular reading problems; with whole group reading, the entire class will read the same text, and the teacher will incorporate activities to help students learn phonics, comprehension, fluency, and vocabulary. In addition to these components of balanced literacy, teachers incorporate writing so that students can learn the structures of communicating through text.

<u>What can teachers expect in their students' literacy development? Are there benchmarks that can be expected by age?</u>

The answer to these questions is fuzzy. While teachers can anticipate that certain skills can be mastered by certain ages, all children are different. When development is too far off the general target then intervention may be necessary.

By their first year, babies can identify words and notice the social and directive impacts of language. By their second year, children have decent vocabularies, make-believe that they are reading books (especially if their role models read), and they can follow simple oral stories. By their third year, children have more advanced skills in listening and speaking. Within the next few years, children are capable of using longer sentences, retelling parts of stories, counting, and "scribbling" messages. They are capable of learning the basics of phonemic awareness. (See http://www.learningpt.org/pdfs/literacy/readingbirthtofive.pdf for more detailed information)

At about five years old, children are really ready to begin learning phonics. Many teachers mistake phonics as being just a step in the process toward comprehension, when in fact, children are fully capable of learning how to comprehend and make meaning at the same age. Phonics, though, ideally will be mastered by second to third grade.

Skill 8.2 Identify instructional methods and strategies for developing and using content area vocabulary.

Content area vocabulary is the specific vocabulary related to particular concepts of various academic disciplines (social science, science, math, art, etc). While teachers tend to think of content area vocabulary as something that should just be focused on at the secondary level (middle and high school), even elementary school-aged students studying various subjects will understand concepts better when the vocabulary used to describe them is explicitly explained. But it is true that in the secondary level, where students go to teachers for the various subjects, content area vocabulary becomes more emphasized.

Often, educators believe that vocabulary should just be taught in the Language Arts class, not realizing that (a) there is not enough time for students to learn the enormous vocabulary in order to be successful with a standards-based education, and (b) that the teaching of vocabulary, related to a particular subject, is a very good way to help students understand the subject better.

How should content area teachers teach vocabulary? First and foremost, teachers should teach students strategies to determine the meanings for difficulty vocabulary when they encounter it on their own. Teachers can do this by teaching students how to identify the meanings of words in context (usually through activities where the word is taken out, and the students have to figure out a way to make sense of the sentence). In addition, dictionary skills must be taught in all subject areas. Teachers should also consider teaching vocabulary is not just the teaching of words: rather, it is the teaching of complex concepts, each with histories and connotations.

When teachers explicitly teach vocabulary, it is best if they can connect new words to words, ideas, and experiences with which students are already familiar. This will help to reduce the strangeness of the new words. Furthermore, the more concrete the examples, the more likely students will be to use the word in context.

Finally, students need plenty of exposure to the new words. They need to be able to hear and use the new words in many naturally-produced sentences. The more one hears and uses a sentence in context, the more the word is solidified in the person's long-term vocabulary.

Skill 8.3 Identify instructional methods to facilitate students' reading comprehension (e.g., summarizing, monitoring comprehension, question answering, question generating, using graphic and semantic organizers, recognizing text structure, and using multiple strategy instruction) throughout the content areas.

The point of comprehension instruction is not necessarily to focus just on the text(s) students are using at the very moment of instruction, but rather to help them learn the strategies that they can use independently with any other text.

Some of the most common methods of teaching instruction are as follows:

Summarization: This is where, either in writing or verbally, students go over the main point of the text, along with strategically chosen details that highlight the main point. This is not the same as *paraphrasing*, which is saying the same thing in different words. Teaching students how to summarize is very important as it will help them look for the most critical areas in a text, and in non-fiction. For example, it will help them distinguish between main arguments and examples. In fiction, it helps students to learn how to focus on the main characters and events and distinguish those from the lesser characters and events.

Question answering: While this tends to be over-used in many classrooms, it is still a valid method of teaching students to comprehend. As the name implies, students answer questions regarding a text, either out loud, in small groups, or individually on paper. The best questions are those that cause students to have to think about the text (rather than just find an answer within the text).

Question generating: This is the opposite of question answering, although students can then be asked to answer their own questions or the questions of peer students. In general, we want students to constantly question texts as they read. This is important because it causes students to become more critical readers. To teach students to generate questions helps them to learn the types of questions they can ask, and it gets them thinking about how best to be critical of texts.

<u>Graphic organizers</u>: Graphic organizers are graphical representations of content within a text. For example, Venn Diagrams can be used to highlight the difference between two characters in a novel or two similar political concepts in a Social Studies textbook. A teacher can use flow-charts with students to talk about the steps in a process (for example, the steps of setting up a science experiment or the chronological events of a story). Semantic organizers are similar in that they graphically display information. The difference, usually, is that semantic organizers focus on words or concepts. For example, a word web can help students make sense of a word by mapping from the central word all the similar and related concepts to that word.

<u>Text structure</u>: Often in non-fiction, particularly in textbooks, and sometimes in fiction, text structures will give important clues to readers about what to look for to find the information they require. Often, students do not know how to make sense of all the types of headings in a textbook and do not realize that, for example, the side-bar story about a character in history is not the main text on a particular page in the history textbook. Teaching students how to interpret text structures gives them tools in which to tackle other similar texts.

<u>Monitoring comprehension</u>: Students need to be aware of their comprehension, or lack of it, in particular texts. So, it is important to teach students what to do when suddenly text stops making sense. For example, students can go back and re-read the description of a character. Or, they can go back to the table of contents or the first paragraph of a chapter to see where they are headed.

<u>Textual marking</u>: This is where students interact with the text as they read. For example, armed with Post-it Notes, students can insert questions or comments regarding specific sentences or paragraphs within the text. This helps students to focus on the importance of the small things, particularly when they are reading larger works (such as novels in high school). It also gives students a reference point on which to go back into the text when they need to review something.

<u>Discussion</u>: Small group or whole-class discussion stimulates thoughts about texts and gives students a larger picture of the impact of those texts. For example, teachers can strategically encourage students to discuss related concepts to the text. This helps students learn to consider texts within larger societal and social concepts, or teachers can encourage students to provide personal opinions in discussion. By listening to various students' opinions, this will help all students in a class to see the wide range of possible interpretations and thoughts regarding one text.

Many people mistakenly believe that the terms "research-based," "research-validated," or "evidence-based" relate mainly to specific programs, such as early reading textbook programs. While research does validate that some of these programs are effective, much research has been conducted regarding the effectiveness of particular instructional strategies.

In reading, many of these strategies have been documented in the report from the National Reading Panel (2000). However, just because a strategy has not been validated as effective by research does not necessarily mean that it is not effective with certain students in certain situations. The number of strategies out there far outweighs researchers' ability to test their effectiveness. Some of the strategies listed above have been validated by rigorous research, while others have been shown consistently to help improve students' reading abilities in localized situations. There simply is not enough space to list all the strategies out there that have been proven effective; just know that the above strategies are very commonly cited ones that work in a variety of situations.

Skill 8.4 Identify strategies for developing critical thinking skills (e.g., analysis, synthesis, evaluation).

Developing critical thinking skills in students is not as simple as teaching some of the more basic skills. In fact, many teachers mistakenly believe these skills can be taught out of context (i.e., they can be taught as skills in and of themselves). Good teachers, however, realize that critical thinking skills must be taught within the contexts of specific subject matter. For example, Language Arts teachers can teach critical thinking skills through novels; Social Studies teachers can teach critical thinking skills through primary source documents or current events; Science teachers can teach critical thinking skills by having students develop hypotheses prior to conducting experiments.

Analysis:
Analysis is the systematic exploration of a concept, event, term, piece of writing, element of media, or any other complex item. Usually, people think of analysis as the exploration of the parts that make up a whole. For example, when someone analyzes a piece of literature, that person might focus on small pieces of the literature; yet, as they focus on the small pieces, they also call attention to the big picture to show how the small pieces create significance for the whole novel.

To carry this example further, if one were to analyze a novel, that person might investigate a particular character to determine how that character adds significance to the whole novel. In something more concrete like biology, one could analyze the findings of an experiment to see if the results might indicate significance for something even larger than the experiment itself. It is very easy to analyze political events, for example. A social studies teacher could ask students to analyze the events leading up to World War II: doing so would require that students look at the small pieces (e.g., smaller world events prior to World War II) and determine how those small pieces, when added up together, caused the war.

Synthesis:
Synthesis is usually thought of as the opposite of analysis. In analysis, the students take a whole and break it up into pieces and examine the pieces. With synthesis, the students examine pieces to try to achieve at a whole relationship. For example, a Language Arts teacher could ask students to synthesize two works of distinct literature. For example: *The Scarlett Letter* and *The Crucible*, two works both featuring life during Puritanical America, written about one century apart. A student could synthesize the two works and come to conclusions about Puritanical life. An Art teacher could ask students to synthesize two paintings from the Impressionist era and come to conclusions about the features that distinguish that style of art.

Evaluation:
Evaluation involves making judgments. Whereas analysis and synthesis seek answers and hypotheses based on investigations, evaluation seeks opinions. For example, a social studies teacher might ask students to evaluate the quality of Richard Nixon's resignation speech. To do so, they would judge whether or not they felt it was a well written and delivered speech. In contrast, analysis would keep judgment out of the assignment: it would have students focus possibly on the structure of the speech (i.e., Does an argument move from emotional to logical?). When evaluating a speech, a piece of literature, a movie, or a work of art, we seek to determine whether one thinks it is good or not.

But, keep in mind, teaching good evaluation skills requires students to learn how to determine whether something is good or not—it requires that they learn how to support their evaluations. So, if a student claims that Nixon's speech was effective in what the President intended the speech to do, the student would need to explain their reasons behind this thinking. Notice that evaluation will probably utilize the skills of analysis and/or synthesis, but that the purpose is ultimately different.

In general, critical thinking skills should be taught through assignments, activities, lessons, and discussions that cause students to think on their own. While teachers can and should provide students with the tools to think critically, they will ultimately become critical thinkers if they have to use those tools themselves. But, this one last point cannot be taken lightly:

Teachers must provide students the tools to evaluate, analyze, and synthesize. Let's take political speeches as an example. Students will be better analyzers, synthesizers, and evaluators if they understand some of the basics of political speeches. Therefore, a teacher might introduce concepts such as rhetoric, style, persona, audience, diction, imagery, and tone. The best way to introduce these concepts would be to provide students with multiple, good examples of these things. Once they are familiar with these critical tools, students will be in a better place to apply them individually to political speeches—and then be able to analyze, synthesize, and evaluate political speeches on their own.

Skill 8.5 Identify appropriate references, materials, and technologies for the subject and the students' abilities.

Over the last few decades, research has confirmed that students do not all learn in the same way. Furthermore, it has bee found that a steady diet of lecture and textbook reading is an extremely ineffective method of instruction. While students definitely should be exposed to lecture and textbooks, they will greatly benefit with the creativity and ingenuity of teachers who find outside resources to assist in the presentation of new knowledge.

Some possibilities outside of the realm of lecture include: textual and media references, hands-on materials, and technology. Lately, teachers have referred to the concept of *multiple texts* as a method of bringing into the classroom multiple types of texts. For example, a social studies teacher might ask students to read an historical novel to complement a unit of study.

In addition to texts, appropriately selected video or audio recordings may be useful. For example, a science teacher may wish to show a short clip of a video that demonstrates how to conduct a particular experiment before students complete the experiment on their own. A language arts teacher may bring in an audio recording of a book to present a uniquely dramatized reading of the book.

Hands-on materials are very important to student learning. For example, math teachers may introduce geometric principles with quilt blocks. The very idea of a science experiment is that hands-on materials and activities more quickly convey scientific ideas to students than do lectures and textbooks.

Finally, technologies, such as personal computers, are very important for student learning. First, it is extremely important that students learn new technologies so that they are able to easily adapt to the myriad of uses found in business and industry. Second, technology can provide knowledge resources that go beyond what a school library, for example, may be able to offer. Students will need to learn how to search for, evaluate, and utilize appropriate information in the internet.

Skill 8.6 Identify methods for differentiating instruction based on student reading data.

Differentiation of instruction occurs when the teacher will vary the content, process, or product (Tomlinson, 1995) used in instruction.

There are three primary ways to differentiate:

- Content – The specifics of what is learned. This does not mean that whole units or concepts should be modified. However, within certain topics, specifics can be modified.
- Process – The route to learning the content. This means that not everyone has to learn the content in exactly the same method.
- Product – The result of the learning. Usually, a product is the end result or assessment of learning. For example, not all students are going to demonstrate complete learning on a quiz; likewise, not all students will demonstrate complete learning on a written paper.

There are two keys to successful differentiation:

- Knowing what is essential in the curriculum. Although certain things can be modified, other things must remain in-tact in a specific order. Disrupting central components of a curriculum can actually damage a student's ability to learn something successfully.
- Knowing the needs of the students. While this can take quite some time to figure out, it is very important that teachers pay attention to the interests, tendencies, and abilities of their students so that they understand how each of their students will best learn.

Many students will need certain concepts explained in greater depth; others may pick up on concepts rather quickly. For this reason, teachers will want to adapt the curriculum in a way that allows students with the opportunity to learn at their own pace, while also keeping the class together as a community. While this can be difficult, the more creative a teacher is with the ways in which students can demonstrate mastery, the more fun the experience will be for students and teachers. Furthermore, teachers will reach students more successfully as they will tailor lesson plans, activities, groupings, and other elements of curriculum to each student's need. The reasons for differentiating instruction are based on two important differences in children: interest and ability.

Differentiating reading instruction is a bit complex. Usually, when a teacher wants to ensure that each student in his or her class is getting the most out of the reading instruction, the teacher will need to consider the level at which the student is proficient in reading—as well as the specific areas that each student struggles. It is first important to use a variety of sources of data to make decisions on differentiation, rather than rely on just one test, for example.

When teachers have proficient readers in their classrooms, they usually feel that these students need less attention and less work. This is wrong. If these students are not provided appropriate instruction and challenging activities to increase their reading abilities further, they may become disengaged with school. These students benefit greatly from integrating classroom reading with other types of reading, perhaps complementing the whole-class novel with some additional short stories or non-fiction pieces.

They also benefit from sustained silent reading, in which they can choose their own books and read independently. Discussion groups and teacher-led discussion activities are also very useful for these students. It is important, however, to ensure that these students do not feel that they have to do extra work than everyone else. Remember, differentiation does not distinguish differences in quantity; it distinguishes differences in type of work.

Average readers may benefit from many of the things that highly proficient readers should do; however, they may need more skill instruction. Most likely, they will not need as much skill instruction as weak readers, but they will benefit highly from having a teacher who knows which skills they are lacking and teaches them to use those skills in their own reading.

Weak readers need to focus highly on skills. Teachers will want to encourage them to make predictions, connect ideas, outline concepts, evaluate, and summarize. The activities that these students engage in should be developed for the purpose of instilling reading strategies that they can use in their independent reading, as well as to propel them toward higher levels of reading.

Competency 9.0   Knowledge of strategies to create and sustain a safe, efficient, supportive learning environment.

Skill 9.1 Evaluate the appropriateness of the physical environment for facilitating student learning and promoting safety.

The physical setting of the classroom contributes a great deal toward the propensity for students to learn. An adequate, well-built, and well-equipped classroom will invite students to learn. This has been called "invitational learning." Among the important factors to consider in the physical setting of the classroom are the following:

- o Adequate physical space
- o Repair status
- o Lighting adequacy
- o Adequate entry/exit access (including handicap accessibility)
- o Ventilation/climate control
- o Coloration

A classroom must have adequate physical space so students can conduct themselves comfortably. Some students are distracted by windows, pencil sharpeners, doors, etc. Some students prefer the front, middle, or back rows.

The teacher has the responsibility to report any items of classroom disrepair to maintenance staff. Broken windows, falling plaster, exposed sharp surfaces, leaks in ceiling or walls, and other items of disrepair present hazards to students.

Another factor which must be considered is adequate lighting. Report any inadequacies in classroom illumination. Florescent lights placed at acute angles often burn out faster. A healthy supply of spare tubes is a sound investment.

Local fire and safety codes dictate entry and exit standards. In addition, all corridors and classrooms should be wheelchair accessible for students and others who use them. Older schools may not have this accessibility.

Another consideration is adequate ventilation and climate control. Some classrooms in some states use air conditioning extensively. Sometimes it is so cold as to be considered a distraction. Specialty classes such as science require specialized hoods for ventilation. Physical Education classes have the added responsibility for shower areas and specialized environments that must be heated such as pool or athletic training rooms.

Classrooms with warmer subdued colors contribute to students' concentration on task items. Neutral hues for coloration of walls, ceiling, and carpet or tile are generally used in classrooms so distraction due to classroom coloration may be minimized.

In the modern classroom, there is a great deal of furniture, equipment, supplies, appliances, and learning aids to help the teacher teach and students learn. The classroom should be provided with furnishings that fit the purpose of the classroom. The kindergarten classroom may have a reading center, a playhouse, a puzzle table, student work desks/tables, a sandbox, and any other relevant learning/interest areas.

Whatever the arrangement of furniture and equipment may be the teacher must provide for adequate traffic flow. Rows of desks must have adequate space between them for students to move and for the teacher to circulate. All areas must be open to line-of-sight supervision by the teacher.

In all cases, proper care must be taken to ensure student safety. Furniture and equipment should be situated safely at all times. No equipment, materials, boxes, etc. should be placed where there is danger of falling. Doors must have entry and exit accessibility at all times.

The major emergency responses include two categories for student movement: tornado warning response; and building evacuation, which includes most other emergencies (fire, bomb threat, etc.). For tornadoes, the prescribed response is to evacuate all students and personnel to the first floor of multi-story buildings, and to place students along walls away from windows. All persons, including the teacher, should then crouch on the floor and cover their heads with their hands. These are standard procedures for severe weather, particularly tornadoes.

Most other emergency situations require evacuation of the school building. Teachers should be thoroughly familiar with evacuation routes established for each classroom in which they teach. Teachers should accompany and supervise students throughout the evacuation procedure, and check to see that all students under their supervision are accounted for. Teachers should then continue to supervise students until the building may be reoccupied (upon proper school or community authority), or until other procedures are followed for students to officially leave the school area and cease to be the supervisory responsibility of the school. Elementary students evacuated to another school can wear nametags and parents or guardians should sign them out at a central location.

Skill 9.2 Identify a repertoire of techniques for establishing smooth, efficient, and well-paced routines.

Effective teachers use class time efficiently. This results in higher student subject engagement and will likely result in more subject matter retention. One way teachers use class time efficiently is through a smooth transition from one activity to another; this is also known as management transition.

Punctuality is a part of management of the classroom time. Punctuality can be defined within a classroom setting as beginning class work/activities promptly. Punctuality can be important as if a class is delayed for ten minutes, over the school year, almost two months of instructional time is lost. Therefore, it is very important to be cognizant of making the most of instructional time.

Management transition is defined as "teacher shifts from one activity to another in a systemic, academically oriented way." One factor that contributes to efficient management transition is the teacher's management of instructional material. Effective teachers gather their materials during the planning stage of instruction. Doing this, a teacher avoids flipping through things and looking for the items necessary for the current lesson. Momentum is lost and student concentration is broken when this occurs.

Additionally, teachers who keep students informed of the sequencing of instructional activities maintain systematic transitions because the students are prepared to move on to the next activity. For example, the teacher says, "When we finish with this guided practice together, we will turn to page twenty-three and each student will do the exercises. I will then circulate throughout the classroom helping on an individual basis. Okay, let's begin." Following an example such as this will lead to systematic smooth transitions between activities because the students will be turning to page twenty-three when the class finishes the practice without a break in concentration.

Another method that leads to smooth transitions is to move students in groups and clusters rather than one by one. This is called *group fragmentation*. For example, if some students do seat work while other students gather for a reading group, the teacher moves the students in pre-determined groups. Instead of calling the individual names of the reading group, which would be time consuming and laborious, the teacher simply says, "Will the blue reading group please assemble at the reading station. The red and yellow groups will quietly do the vocabulary assignment I am now passing out." As a result of this activity, the classroom is ready to move on in a matter of seconds rather than minutes.

Additionally, the teacher may employ academic transition signals, defined as "teacher utterance that indicate[s] movement of the lesson from one topic or activity to another by indicating where the lesson is and where it is going." For example, the teacher may say, "That completes our description of clouds, now we will examine weather fronts." Like the sequencing of instructional materials, this keeps the student informed on what is coming next so the students will move to the next activity with little or no break in concentration.

Therefore, effective teachers manage transitions from one activity to another in a systematically oriented way through efficient management of instructional matter, sequencing of instructional activities, moving students in groups and by employing academic transition signals. Through an efficient use of class time, achievement is increased because students spend more class time engaged in on-task behavior.

Transition refers to changes in class activities that involve movement. Examples are:
- Breaking up from large group instruction into small groups for learning centers and small-group instructions
- Classroom to lunch, to the playground, or to elective classes
- Finishing reading at the end of one period and getting ready for math the next period
- Emergency situations such as fire drills

Successful transitions are achieved by using proactive strategies. Early in the year, the teacher pinpoints the transition periods in the day and anticipates possible behavior problems, such as students habitually returning late from lunch. After identifying possible problems with the environment or the schedule, the teacher plans proactive strategies to minimize or eliminate those problems.

Proactive planning also gives the teacher the advantage of being prepared, addressing behaviors before they become problems, and incorporating strategies into the classroom management plan right away. Transition plans can be developed for each type of transition and the expected behaviors for each situation taught directly to the students.

Skill 9.3 Identify strategies to involve students in establishing rules and standards for behavior.

Teaching social skills can be rather difficult because social competence requires a repertoire of skills in a number of areas. The socially competent person must be able to get along with family and friends, function in a work environment, take care of personal needs, solve problems in daily living, and identify sources of help. A class of students with emotional disabilities may present several deficits in a few areas or a few deficits in many areas. Therefore, the teacher must begin with an assessment of the skill deficits and prioritize the ones to teach first.

Type of Assessment	Description
Direct Observation	Observe student in various settings with a checklist
Role Play	Teacher observes students in structured scenarios
Teacher Ratings	Teacher rates student with a checklist or formal assessment instrument
Sociometric Measures: Peer Nomination	Student names specific classmates who meet a stated criterion (i.e., playmate). Score is the number of times a child is nominated.
Peer Rating	Students rank all their classmates on a Likert-type scale (e.g., 1-3 or 1-5 scale) on stated criterion. Individual score is the average of the total ratings of their classmates.
Paired-Comparison	Student is presented with paired classmate combinations and asked to choose who is most or least liked in the pair.
Context Observation	Student is observed to determine if the skill deficit is present in one setting, but not others
Comparison with other student	Student's social skill behavior is compared to two other students in the same situation to determine if there is a deficit, or if the behavior is not really a problem.

Social skills instruction can include teaching conversation skills, assertiveness, play and peer interaction, problem solving and coping skills, self-help, task-related behaviors, self-concept related skills (i.e., expressing feelings, accepting consequences), and job related skills.

One advantage of schooling organizations for students is to facilitate social skills and social development. While teachers cannot take the largest role for developing such traits as honesty, fairness, and concern for others, they are extremely important in the process. The first recommendation is to be a very good role model. As we all know, actions do indeed speak louder than words.

Second, teachers need to communicate expectations and be firm about them. When teachers ignore certain "infractions" and make a big deal about others, they demonstrate to students that it isn't about manners and social skills, but rather discipline and favoritism. All students need to feel safe, cared about, and secure with their classmates. Teachers are the best people to ensure that students understand how to be generous, caring, considerate, and sociable individuals.

Behavior Management Plan Strategies for Increasing Desired Behaviors

1. **Prompt**-A prompt is a visual or verbal cue that assists the child through the behavior shaping process. In some cases, the teacher may use a physical prompt such as guiding a child's hand. Visual cues include signs or other visual aids. Verbal cues include talking a child through the steps of a task. The gradual removal of the prompt as the child masters the target behavior is called *fading*.

2. **Modeling**-In order for modeling to be effective, the child must be at a cognitive and developmental level to imitate the model. Teachers are behavior models in the classroom, but peers are powerful models as well, especially in adolescence. A child who does not perceive a model as acceptable will not likely copy the model's behavior. This is why teachers should be careful to reinforce appropriate behavior and not fall into the trap of attending to inappropriate behaviors. Children who see that the students who misbehave get the teacher's constant attention will most likely begin to model those students' behaviors.

3. **Contingency Contracting**-Also known as the *Premack Principle* or *"Grandma's Law"*, this technique is based on the concept that a preferred behavior which frequently occurs can be used to increase a less preferred behavior with a low rate of occurrence. In short, performance of X results in the opportunity to do Y, such as getting 10 minutes of free time for completing the math assignment with 85% accuracy.

Contingency contracts are a process that continues after formal schooling and into the world of work and adult living. Contracts can be individualized, developed with input of the child, and accent positive behaviors. Contingencies can also be simple verbal contracts, such as the teacher telling a child that he or she may earn a treat or special activity for completion of a specific academic activity. Contingency contracts can be simple daily contracts or more formal, written contracts.

Written contracts last for longer periods of time, and must be clear, specific, and fair. Payoffs should be deliverable immediately after the student completes the terms of the contract. An advantage of a written contract is the child can see and re-affirm the terms of the contract. By being actively involved in the development of the contract with the teacher and/or parent, the child assumes responsibility for fulfilling his share of the deal. Contracts can be renewed and renegotiated as the student progresses toward the target behavior goal.

4. **Token Economy**-A token economy mirrors the money system in that the students earn tokens (money) which are of little value in themselves, but can be traded for tangible or activity rewards, just as currency can be spent for merchandise. Using stamps, stickers, stars, or point cards instead of items like poker chips decrease the likelihood of theft, loss, and noise in the classroom.

Tips for a token economy:
- Keep the system simple to understand and administer
- Develop a reward "menu" which is deliverable and varied
- Decide on the target behaviors
- Explain the system completely and in positive terms before beginning the economy
- Periodically review the rules
- Price the rewards and costs fairly, and post the menu where it will be easily read
- Gradually fade to a variable schedule of reinforcement

Behavior Management Plan Strategies for Decreasing Undesirable Behaviors:

1. Extinction-Reinforcement is withheld for an unacceptable behavior. A common example is ignoring the student who calls out without raising his hand and recognizing the student who is raising his hand to speak. This would not be a suitable strategy for serious misbehaviors where others are in danger of being hurt.

2. Differential Reinforcement of Incompatible Behaviors (DRI)-In this method, the teacher reinforces an acceptable behavior that is not compatible with the target behavior. A child cannot be out of her seat and in her seat at the same time, so the teacher would reinforce the time when the child is in her seat.

3. Differential Reinforcement of Alternative Behaviors (DRA)-Student is reinforced for producing a behavior that is an alternative to the undesired target behavior, such as talking with a classmate instead of arguing.

4. Differential Reinforcement of Other Behaviors (DRO)-Reinforcement is provided for producing any appropriate behaviors except for the target behavior during a specified time interval. This technique works well with stereotypic, disruptive, or self-injurious behaviors.

5. Satiation or Negative Practice-This technique involves reinforcing the inappropriate behavior on a fixed reinforcement schedule until the student discontinues the behavior. The reinforcement must be consistently applied until the student does not want to do it. Behaviors suitable for satiation would be chronic "borrowing" of school supplies, getting up to go to the wastebasket or pencil sharpener, or asking for the time. An example would be giving a student a pencil to sharpen at frequent intervals throughout the day so that the act of getting up to sharpen a pencil no longer has any appeal.

6. Verbal Reprimands-Reprimands are best delivered privately, especially for secondary students, who may be provoked into more misbehavior if they are embarrassed in front of their peers. Verbal reprimands also may be a source of attention and reinforcement with some students.

Punishment as a " Deterrent" to Misbehavior

Punishment should **not** be the first strategy in behavior management plans because it tends to suppress behavior, not eliminate it. Punishment focuses on the negative rather than positive behaviors. There is also the chance that the child will comply out of fear, stress, or tension rather than a genuine behavior change. Furthermore, there is the chance that punishment may be misused to the point where it is no longer effective. Forms of punishment include:

1. **Adding an aversive event** (i.e., detention, lunchroom cleanup, extra assignments)

2. **Subtracting something that the child likes** (i.e., recess)

   a. **Response Cost-**In token economies, response cost results in loss of points or token. Response-cost or loss of privileges is preferred to adding aversives, but for long-term changes in behavior, punishment is less effective than other forms of decreasing misbehavior, such as extinction and ignoring.

b. **Time-Out-**Time-out is removing a child from the reinforcing situation to a setting that is not reinforcing. Time out may be **observational** (i.e., sitting at the end of the basketball court for five minutes or putting one's head down at the desk). The point is to have the child observe the others engaging in the appropriate behavior.

   i. **Exclusion time-out-** involves placing a visual barrier between the student and the rest of the class. This could be a divider between the desks and the time-out area, or removing the child to another room.

   ii. **Seclusion time-out** -necessitates a special time-out room that adheres to mandated standards, as well as a log of the children who are taken to time out, the reasons, and the time spent there.

In order to be effective, time-out must be consistently applied, and the child must understand why he is being sent to the time out area and for how long. The teacher briefly explains the reason for time-out, directs the child to the area, and refrains from long explanations, arguments, or debates. The time-out area should be as neutral as possible, away from busy areas, and easily observed by the monitor, but not from the rest of the class. The duration of time-out should vary with the age of the child, and timed so the child knows when the end of time-out has arrived.

Time-out as part of a behavior management plan needs to be periodically evaluated for its effectiveness. By analyzing records of time-out (as required and directed by the school district), the teacher can see if the technique is working. If a student regularly goes to time-out at a certain time, the student may be avoiding a frustrating situation or a difficult academic subject. Seclusion time out may be effective for children who tend to be group-oriented, acting-out, or aggressive. Isolation from the group is not rewarding for them. Shy, solitary, or withdrawn children may actually prefer to be in time-out and increase the target behavior in order to go to time-out.

3. **Overcorrection -** Overcorrection is more effective with severe and profoundly handicapped students. The student is required to repeat an appropriate behavior for a specified number of times when the inappropriate behavior is exhibited.

4. **Suspension -** Suspension is the punishment of last resort. In addition to restrictions on suspension for students with disabilities, suspension translates into a "vacation" from school for many students with behavioral problems. Furthermore, suspension does not relieve the teacher from the responsibility of exploring alternatives that may be effective with the child. An alternative to out-of-school suspension is in-school suspension, where the student is placed in a special area to do his or her class work for a specified time and with minimal privileges. Extended suspensions (i.e., for drugs, weapons, or assault) or offenses punishable by expulsion result in a change of placement, which calls for special meetings to discuss alternative placement and/or services

Group-Oriented Contingencies in Behavior Management

This strategy uses the power of the peer group to reinforce appropriate behavior. In one variation, *dependent group-oriented contingencies*, the rewards of consequences for the entire group depend upon the performance of a few members. Example: Susan's class receives a candy reward if she does not have a crying outburst for two days.

Interdependent group-oriented contingencies mean that each member of the group must achieve a specified level of performance in order for the group to get the reward. An example would be the entire class earning one period of free time if everyone passes the science test with at least 80%.

Other Strategies for Behavior Management

1. **Counseling Techniques -**These techniques include life-space interview, reality therapy, and active listening.

2. **Consequences-** Consequences should be as close as possible to the outside world, especially for adolescents.

3. **Student Participation-** Students, especially older students, should participate as much as possible in the planning, goal setting, and evaluation of their behavior management plans.

4. **Contingency Plans -** Because adolescents frequently have a number of reinforcers outside of school, the teacher should try to incorporate contingencies for school behavior at home, since parents can control important reinforcers such as movies, going out with friends, car privileges, etc.

5. **Consistency** -Consistency, especially with adolescents, reduces the occurrence of power struggles and teaches them that predictable consequences follow for their choice of actions.

Initially, the target behavior may increase or worsen as the student realizes that the behavior no longer is reinforced. However, if the behavior management plan is properly administered, the teacher should begin to see results. Behavior management plan evaluation is a continuous process, since changes in behavior require changes in the target behavior, looking for outside variables that may account for behavior change, or changes in reinforcement schedules and menus.

It has already been established that appropriate verbal techniques include a soft non-threatening voice, avoidance of undue roughness, anger, or impatience regardless of whether the teacher is instructing, providing student alert, or giving a behavior reprimand.

Verbal techniques, which may be effective in modifying student behavior, include simply stating the student's name, explaining briefly and succinctly what the student is doing that is inappropriate and what the student should be doing. Verbal techniques for reinforcing behavior include both encouragement and praise delivered by the teacher.

In addition, for verbal techniques to positively effect student behavior and learning, the teacher must give clear, concise directives while implying her warmth toward the students.

Other factors that contribute to enhanced student learning have to do with body language. The teacher needs to make eye contact with individual students, smile and nod approvingly, move closer to the students, give gentle pats on the shoulder, arm or head, and bend over so that the teacher is face to face with the children.

Some of these same techniques can be applied as a means of desisting student misbehaviors. Rather than smiling, the teacher may need to make eye contact first and then nod disapprovingly. Again a gentle tap on the shoulder or arm can be used to get a student's attention in an attempt to stop deviancy.

It is also helpful for the teacher to display prominently the classroom rules. This will serve as a visual reminder of the students' expected behaviors. In a study of classroom management procedures, it was established that the combination of conspicuously displayed rules, frequent verbal references to the rules, and appropriate consequences for appropriate behaviors led to increased levels of on-task behavior.

Skill 9.4 Identify emergency procedures for student and campus safety.

Statutes state only the following with regard to school emergencies:

235.14 Emergency drills.—The Department of Education shall formulate and prescribe rules and instructions for emergency drills for all the public schools of the state which comprise grades K-12 and for the School for the Deaf and the Blind. Each administrator or teacher in charge of such a facility shall be provided a copy of the rules and instructions; and each such person shall see that such emergency drills are held at least once each calendar quarter and that all personnel and students are properly instructed regarding such rules and instructions.

This statute addresses instructions for drills only, not for actual emergency procedures. Among the possible emergencies that have been identified which schools might face are fire, flood, tornado, bomb threat, chemical accident, traffic related chemical spills (i.e. Boynton Beach, FL, 1996), earthquake and hurricanes. The primary concern in emergency situations is the physical safety and well being of students. The teacher must be thoroughly familiar with the prescribed movement of students in emergency situations in order to minimize danger to the students and to other school personnel.

The major emergency responses include two categories for student movement: tornado warning response; and building evacuation, which includes most other emergencies (fire, bomb threat, etc.). For tornadoes, the prescribed response is to evacuate all students and personnel to the first floor of multi-story buildings, and to place students along walls away from windows.

All persons, including the teacher, should then crouch on the floor and cover their heads with their hands. These are standard procedures for severe weather, particularly tornadoes.

Most other emergency situations require evacuation of the school building. Teachers should be thoroughly familiar with evacuation routes established for each classroom in which they teach. Teachers should accompany and supervise students throughout the evacuation procedure, and check to see that all students under their supervision are accounted for. Teachers should then continue to supervise students until the building may be reoccupied (upon proper school or community authority), or until other procedures are followed for students to officially leave the school area and cease to be the supervisory responsibility of the school. Elementary students evacuated to another school can wear nametags and parents or guardians should sign them out at a central location.

Competency 10.0 Knowledge of how to plan and conduct lessons in a variety of learning environments that lead to student outcomes consistent with state and district standards.

Skill 10.1 Determine instructional long-term goals and short-term objectives appropriate to student needs.

Once long range goals have been identified and established, it is important to ensure that all goals and objectives are also in conjunction with student ability and needs. Some objectives may be too basic for a higher level student, while others cannot be met with a student's current level of knowledge. There are many forms of evaluating student needs to ensure that all goals set are challenging yet achievable.

Teachers should check a student's cumulative file, located in guidance, for reading level and prior subject area achievement. This provides a basis for goal setting but shouldn't be the only method used. Depending on the subject area, basic skills test, reading level evaluations, writing samples, and/or interest surveys can all be useful in determining if all goals are appropriate. Informal observation should always be used as well. Finally, it is important to take into consideration the student's level of motivation when addressing student needs.

When given objectives by the school or county, teachers may wish to adapt them so that they can better meet the needs of their individual student population. For example, if a high level advanced class is given the objective, "*State five causes of World War II,*" a teacher may wish to adapt the objective to a higher level. "*State five causes of World War II and explain how they contributed to the start of the war.*" Subsequently objectives can be modified for a lower level as well. "*From a list of causes, pick three that specifically caused World War II.*"

When organizing and sequencing objectives the teacher needs toremember that skills are building blocks. A taxonomy of educational objectives can be helpful to construct and organize objectives. Knowledge of material, for example, memorizing definitions or famous quotes, is low on the taxonomy of learning and should be worked with early in the sequence of teaching.. Eventually, objectives should be developed to include higher level thinking such as comprehension (i.e., being able to use a definition); application (i.e., being able to apply the definition to other situations); synthesis (i.e., being able to add other information); and evaluation (i.e., being able to judge the value of something).

Emergent curriculum describes the projects and themes that classrooms may embark upon that have been inspired by the children's interests. The teacher uses all the tools of assessment available to her to learn as much as she can about her students, and then she continually assesses them over the period of the unit or semester. As she gets to know them, she listens to what their interests are and creates a curriculum in response to what she learns from her observations of her own students.

Webbing is a recent concept related to the idea of emergent curriculum. The two main uses of webbing are planning and recording curriculum. Planning webs are used to generate ideas for activities and projects for the children from an observed interest such as rocks.

Teachers work together to come up with ideas and activities for the children and to record them in on a web format. Activities can be grouped by different areas of the room or by developmental domains. For example, clusters either fall under areas such as dramatic play or science areas or around domains such as language, cognitive, and physical development. Either configuration works; being consistent in each web is important.

This format will work as a unit, weekly, or monthly program plan. Any new activities that emerge throughout the unit can also be added to the web. The record will serve in the future to plan using activities that emerge from the children's play and ideas.

Skill 10.2 Identify activities that support the knowledge, skills, and attitudes to be learned in a given subject area.

As a teacher, it is important to be aware of the skills and information that are pertinent to the subject area being taught. Teachers need to determine what information a student should carry with them at the end of a term. The teacher should also be aware of skills needed to complete any objective for that subject area and determine how skilled their students are at using them.

Because most goals are building blocks, all necessary underlying skills should be determined and a teacher must evaluate if the student has demonstrated these abilities. For example, to do mathematical word problems, students must have a sufficiently high enough level of reading to understand the problem.

Once the desired knowledge, skills and attitudes have been established, a teacher must develop short-range objectives designed to help in the achievement of these outcomes. An objective is a specific learning outcome that is used to achieve long-range goals. Objectives should be stated in observable terms such as: to state, to demonstrate, to list, to complete or to solve. Objectives should be clear and concise (i.e. students will be able to state five causes of World War II).

Skill 10.3 Identify materials based on instructional objectives and student learning needs and performance levels.

In considering suitable learning materials for the classroom, the teacher must have a thorough understanding of the state-mandated competency-based curriculum. According to state requirements, certain objectives must be met in each subject taught at every designated level of instruction. It is necessary that the teacher become well acquainted with the curriculum for which he/she is assigned. The teacher must also be aware that it is unlawful to require students to study from textbooks or materials other than those approved by the State Department of Education.

Keeping in mind the state requirements concerning the objectives and materials, the teacher must determine the abilities of the incoming students assigned to his/her class or supervision. It is essential to be aware of their entry behavior—that is, their current level of achievement in the relevant areas. The next step is to take a broad overview of students who are expected to learn before they are passed on to the next grade or level of instruction. Finally, the teacher must design a course of study that will enable students to reach the necessary level of achievement, as displayed in their final assessments, or exit behaviors. Textbooks and learning materials must be chosen to fit into this context.

To determine the abilities of incoming students, it may be helpful to consult their prior academic records. Letter grades assigned at previous levels of instruction as well as scores on standardized tests may be taken into account. In addition, the teacher may choose to administer pre-tests at the beginning of the school year, and perhaps also at the initial stage of each new unit of instruction. The textbooks available for classroom use may provide suitable pre-tests, tests of student progress, and post-tests.

In selecting tests and other assessment tools, the teacher should keep in mind that different kinds of tests measure different aspects of student development. The tests included in most textbooks chosen for the classroom, and in the teacher's manual that accompanies them are usually achievement tests. Few of these are the type of tests intended to measure the students' inherent ability or aptitude. Teachers will find it difficult to raise students' scores on ability tests, but students' scores on achievement tests may be expected to improve with proper instruction and application in the area being studied.

In addition to administering tests, the teacher may assess the readiness of students for a particular level of instruction by having them demonstrate their ability to perform some relevant task. In a class that emphasizes written composition, for example, students may be asked to submit writing samples.

These may be used not only to assure the placement of the students into the proper level, but as a diagnostic tool to help them understand what aspects of their composition skills may need improvement. In the like manner, students in a speech class may be asked to make an impromptu oral presentation before beginning a new level or specific level of instruction. Others may be asked to demonstrate their psychomotor skills in a physical education class, display their computational skills in a mathematics class, and so on. Whatever the chosen task, the teacher will need to select or devise an appropriate assessment scale and interpret the results with care.

If students are informed their entry behaviors on such a scale, they will be better motivated, especially if they are able to observe their progress by an objective means at suitable intervals during the course. For this reason, it may be advisable to record the results of such assessments in the student's portfolios as well as in the teacher's records.

Teachers may also gauge student readiness by simply asking them about their previous experience or knowledge of the subject or task at hand. While their comments may not be completely reliable indicators of what they know or understand, such discussions have the advantage of providing an idea of the students' interest in what is being taught. Teachers can have little impact unless they are able to demonstrate how the material being introduced is relevant to the students' lives.

Keeping in mind what is understood about the students' abilities and interests, the teacher should design a course of study that presents units of instruction in an orderly sequence. The instruction should be planned so as to advance all students toward the next level of instruction, although exit behaviors need not be identical due to the inevitability of individual differences.

Once students' abilities are determined, the teacher will select the learning materials for the class. In choosing materials, teachers should also keep in mind that not only do students learn at different rates, but they bring a variety of cognitive styles to the learning process. Prior experiences influence the individual's cognitive style, or method of accepting, processing, and retaining information.

Most teachers chose to use textbooks, which are suitable to the age and developmental level of specific student populations. Textbooks reflect the values and assumptions of the society that produces them, while they also represent the knowledge and skills considered to be essential in becoming an educated adult. Finally, textbooks are useful to the school bureaucracy and the community, for they make public and accessible the private world of the classroom.

Though these factors may favor the adoption of textbooks, the individual teacher may have only limited choice about which textbooks to use, since such decisions are often made by the school administration or the local school district (in observance of the state guidelines). If teachers are consulted about textbook selection, it is likely that they have little training in evaluation techniques, and they are seldom granted leave time to encourage informed decisions. On those occasions when teachers are asked to assist in the selection process, they should ask, above all, whether the textbooks have real substance—is World War II accurately chronicled, does the science textbook correctly conceptualize electrical current, do literary selections reflect a full range of genre?

From time to time, controversy has arisen about the possible weakness of textbooks—the preponderance of pictures and illustrations, the avoidance of controversy in social studies textbooks, the lack of emphasis on problem-solving in science books, and so on. In the 1980's, certain books were criticized for their attention to the liberal or secular values, and the creationism/evolution argument has re-surfaced again and again.

Finally, recent decades have witnessed a movement to grant more attention to women, African-Americans, and other groups whose contributions to our developing culture may have been overlooked in earlier textbooks. Individual teachers would be well advised to keep themselves informed of current trends or developments, so as to make better informed choices for their students and deal with the possibility of parental concern.

Focusing on the needs evident in almost any classroom population, the teacher will want to use textbooks that include some of the activities and selections to challenge the most advanced students as well as those who have difficulty in mastering the material at a moderate pace. Some of the exercises may be eliminated altogether for faster learners, while students who have difficulty may need to have material arranged into brief steps or sections.

For almost any class, some experience in co-operative learning may be advisable. Thus, the faster learners will reinforce what they have already mastered, while those of lesser ability at the tasks in question can ask about their individual problems or areas of concern. Most textbook exercises intended for independent work can be used in cooperative learning, though in most cases, teachers will encourage better participation if the cooperating group is asked to hand in a single paper or project to represent their combined efforts, rather than individual papers or projects. This method does not always require that all members of the group be assigned the same grade (If letter grades are assigned at all for such assignments).

Depending on what students have been told before starting the activity, the teacher may be justified in adjusting grades accordingly if s/he observes some students applying more effort than the others to the cooperative learning endeavor.

In choosing materials, teachers should also keep in mind that students learn at different rates, and they bring a variety of cognitive styles to the learning process. Prior experiences influence the individual's cognitive style, or method of accepting, processing, and retaining information. According to Marshall Rosenberg, students can be categorized as:

- Rrigid-inhibited
- Undisciplined
- Acceptance-anxious
- Creative

"The creative learner is an independent thinker, one who maximizes his/her abilities, can work by his/herself, enjoys learning, and is self-critical." This last category constitutes the ideal, but teachers should make every effort to use materials that will stimulate and hold the attention of learners of all types.

Aside from textbooks, there is a wide variety of materials available to today's teachers. Computers are now commonplace, and some schools can now afford DVDs to bring alive the content of a reference book in text, motion, and sound. Hand-held calculators eliminate the need for drill and practice in number facts, while they also support a problem solving and process to mathematics. Videocassettes (VCR's) are common and permit the use of home-produced or commercially produced tapes. Textbook publishers often provide films, recordings, and software to accompany the text, as well as maps, graphics, and colorful posters to help students visualize what is being taught. Teachers can usually scan the educational publishers' brochures that arrive at their principal's or department head's office on a frequent basis. Another way to stay current in the field is by attending workshops or conferences. Teachers will be enthusiastically welcomed on those occasions when educational publishers are asked to display their latest productions and revised editions of materials.

In addition, yesterday's libraries are today's media centers. Teachers can usually have opaque projectors delivered to the classroom to project print or pictorial images (including student work) onto a screen for classroom viewing. Some teachers have chosen to replace chalkboards with projectors that reproduce the print or images present on the plastic sheets known as transparencies, which the teacher can write on during a presentation or have machine-printed in advance. In either case, the transparency can easily be stored for later use. In an art or photography class, or any class in which it is helpful to display visual materials, slides can easily be projected onto a wall or a screen. Cameras are inexpensive enough to enable students to photograph and display their own work, as well as keep a record of their achievements in teacher files or student portfolios.

Competency 11.0   Knowledge of collaborative strategies for working with various education professionals, parents, and other appropriate participants in the continual improvement of educational experiences of students.

Skill 11.1 Identify student behavior indicating possible emotional distress, substance abuse, abuse or neglect, and suicidal tendencies.

All students demonstrate some behaviors that may indicate emotional distress from time to time, since all children experience stressful periods within their lives. However, the emotionally healthy students can maintain control of their own behavior even during stressful times. Teachers need to be mindful that the difference between typical stressful behavior and severe emotional distress is determined by the frequency, duration, and intensity of stressful behavior.

Lying, stealing, and fighting are atypical behaviors that most children may exhibit occasionally, but if a child lies, steals, or fights regularly or blatantly, these behaviors may be indicative of emotional distress. Lying is especially common among young children who feel the need to avoid punishment or as a means to make themselves feel more important.

As children become older, past the ages of six or seven, lying is often a signal that the child is feeling insecure. These feelings of insecurity may escalate to the point of being habitual or obvious and may indicate that the child is seeking attention due to emotional distress. Fighting, especially among siblings, is a common occurrence. However, if a child fights, is unduly aggressive, or is belligerent towards others on a long-term basis, teachers and parents need to consider the possibility of emotional problems.

How can a teacher know when a child needs help with his/her behavior? The child will indicate a need for help with his/her behavior their actions. Breaking rules established by parents, teachers, and other authorities and destroying property can signify that a student is losing control especially when these behaviors occur frequently. Other signs that a child needs help may include frequent bouts of crying, a quarrelsome attitude, and constant complaints about school, friends, or life in general. Anytime a child's disposition, attitude, or habits change significantly, teachers and parents need to seriously consider the existence of emotional difficulties.

Emotional disturbances in childhood are not uncommon and take a variety of forms. Usually these problems show up in the form of uncharacteristic behaviors. Most of the time, children respond favorably to brief treatment programs of psychotherapy. At other times, disturbances may need more intensive therapy and are harder to resolve. All stressful behaviors need to be addressed, and any type of chronic antisocial behavior needs to be examined as a possible symptom of deep-seated emotional upset.

Many safe and helpful interventions are available to the classroom teacher when dealing with a student who is suffering serious emotional disturbances. First, and foremost, the teacher must maintain open communication with the parents and other professionals who are involved with the student whenever overt behavior characteristics are exhibited. Students with behavior disorders need constant behavior modification, which may involve two-way communication between the home and school on a daily basis.

The teacher must establish an environment that promotes appropriate behavior for all students as well as respect for one another. The students may need to be informed of any special needs that their classmates may have so they can give due consideration. The teacher should also initiate a behavior modification program for any student that might show emotional or behavioral disorders. Such behavior modification plans can be effective means of preventing deviant behavior. If deviant behavior does occur, the teacher should have arranged for a safe and secure time-out place where the student can go for a respite and an opportunity to regain self-control prior to the need for such a place.

Often when a behavior disorder is more severe, the student must be involved in a more concentrated program aimed at alleviating deviant behavior such as psychotherapy. In such instances, the school psychologist, guidance counselor, or behavior specialist is directly involved with the student and provides counseling and therapy on a regular basis. Frequently they are also involved with the student's family.

As a last resort, many families are turning to drug therapy. Once viewed as a radical step, administering drugs to children to balance their emotions or control their behavior has become a widely used form of therapy. Of course, only a medical doctor can prescribe such drugs.

Great care must be exercised when giving pills to children in order to change their behavior, especially since so many medicines have undesirable side effects. It is important to know that these drugs relieve only the symptoms of behavior and do not get at the underlying causes. Parents and teachers need to be educated as to the side effects of these medications.

Neurotic Disorders
Sometimes emotional disorders escalate so severely that the child's well-being is threatened. Teachers and parents must recognize the signs of severe emotional stress, which may become detrimental to the child. There are various forms of emotional disorders that can be potentially dangerous including neurotic disorders. Neuroses are the second most common group of psychiatric disturbances of childhood and symptoms include extreme anxiety related to over dependence, social isolation, sleep problems, unwarranted nausea, abdominal pain, diarrhea, or headaches.

Some children show characteristics of irrational fears of particular objects or situations, while others become consumed with obsessions, thoughts, or ideas. One of the most serious neuroses is depression. The child is sad and depressed, crying, showing little or no interest in people or activities, having eating and sleeping problems, and sometimes talking about wanting to be dead. Teachers need to listen to what the child is saying and should take these verbal expressions very seriously.

Psychotic Disorders

An even more serious emotional disorder is psychosis, which is characterized by a loss of contact with reality. Psychosis is rare in childhood but when it does occur, it is often difficult to diagnose. One fairly constant sign is the child's failure to make normal emotional contact with other people. The most common psychosis of childhood is schizophrenia, which is a deliberate escape from reality and a withdrawal from relationships with others. When this syndrome occurs in childhood, the child will continue to have some contact with people; however, there is a curtain between them and the rest of the world. It is more common in boys than in girls. One of the major signs of this disorder is a habitually flat or habitually agitated facial expression. Children suffering from schizophrenia are occasionally mute, but at times they talk incessantly using bizarre words in ways that make no sense. Their incoherent speech often contributes to their frustration and compounds their fears and preoccupation and is the most significant sign of this very serious disturbance.

Early Infantile Autism

This disorder may occur as early as the fourth month of life. Suddenly the infant lies apathetic and oblivious in the crib. In other cases, the baby seems perfectly normal throughout infancy and then the symptoms appear without warning at about eighteen months of age. Due to the nature of the symptoms, autistic children are often misdiagnosed as mentally retarded, deaf-mute, or organically brain-damaged. Autistic children are twice as likely to be boys as girls.

According to many psychologists who have been involved with treating autistic children, it seems that these children have built a wall between themselves and everyone else, including their families and even their parents. They rarely make eye contact with others and do not even appear to hear the voices of those who speak to them. They cannot empathize with others and have no ability to appreciate humor.

Autistic children usually have language disturbances. One third of them never develop speech skills, but may grunt or whine. Others may repeat the same word or phrase over and over or parrot what someone else has said. They often lack even inner language as well and cannot play by themselves above a primitive, sensory-motor level.

Frequently, autistic children will appear to fill the void left by the absence of interpersonal relationships in their lives with a preoccupation with things. They become compulsive about the arrangements of objects and often engage in simple, repetitive physical activities with objects for long periods of time. If these activities are interrupted, they may react with fear or rage. Others remain motionless for hours each day sometimes moving only their eyes or hands.

On intelligence tests, autistic children score from severely subnormal to high average. Some exhibit astonishing ability in isolated skill areas while functioning poorly in general. They may be able to memorize volumes of material, sing beautifully or perform complicated difficult mathematical problems.

The cause of early infantile autism is unknown. Years ago some psychiatrists speculated that these children did not develop normally due to a lack of parental warmth. This has been found to be unlikely since the incidence of autism in families is usually limited to one child. Other theories include metabolic or chromosomal defects as causes; however, there is no proof.

The prognosis for autistic children is painfully discouraging. Only about five percent of autistic children become socially well adjusted in adulthood. Another twenty percent make fair social adjustments. The remaining seventy-five percent are socially incapacitated and must be supervised for the duration of their lives. Treatment may include outpatient psychotherapy, drugs, or long-term treatment in a residential center, but neither the form of treatment nor even the lack of treatment seems to make a difference in the long run.

Drug Abuse:
It is first necessary to clarify abuse vs. dependency. Abuse is a lesser degree of involvement with substances; usually implying the person is not physically addicted. They may have just as many soft signs of involvement, but lack true addiction. Dependency indicates a true physical addiction, characterized by several hard signs, some of which are less likely to be seen in a school setting. The person may experience withdrawal symptoms when deprived of the substance. The person may experience blackouts. They may use more and more of the substance to get the same effect (tolerance). And they will exhibit irresponsible, illogical, and dangerous use of the substance.

Soft signs, declines in functioning, are seen clearly in social, occupational, mental and emotional, and spiritual life. These last symptoms are most likely to be observed by an educator. Because determining addiction is not a concern for the educator, we will use the term abuse in this paper. The difference clinically may be academic for this age group, as addiction occurs at a high rate, and rapidly after first use in young people, sometimes after only a few tries. Legally, any use of an illicit substance for a minor, including alcohol, is automatically considered abuse.

Behaviors Indicating Drug/Alcohol Abuse

Substance abuse of all kinds can be described by the following symptoms: withdrawal syndrome, blackouts, and tolerance. These hard signs of addiction, or dependency, are those that affect physiology:

1. Withdrawal is seen when the substance(s) are removed and various symptoms indicating a metabolic craving are experienced: sweating, nausea, dizziness, elevated blood pressure, seizures, and rarely death.
2. When a substance dependent is seen ambulatory, but later doesn't remember anything of his actions, it's called a blackout. The anesthetized mind has eliminated conscious wakeful activity, functioning mainly on instinct.
3. Tolerance changes over the course of the disease, increasing in the early stages, and decreasing in the late chronic stage.

In the school setting, hard signs of dependency are to be considered very serious. Any student who exhibits hard signs associated with substance ingestion must be treated by medical staff at a medical facility immediately.

Seizures due to withdrawal are fatal 17% of the time and overdoses due to mixed substances or overuse of a single substance are rapidly fatal, including overdoses with alcohol alone. Never, under any circumstances, attempt to treat, protect, tolerate, or negotiate with a student who is showing signs of being in a state of physical crisis. They are to be removed from the school center by EMS or police as soon as possible, and given constant one to one supervision away from the regular classroom before being taken to the hospital. Police must be called as this student is a danger to self or others in their condition. If it is questionable whether one should do the summoning, find out what the protocol is for each step.

Another hard sign is: irresponsible, illogical, and dangerous use. The use of any substance by young people constitutes irresponsible, illogical and dangerous use, if for no other reason than substances of abuse, including alcohol, are all illegal. In the eyes of medical science, there exists a zero level of tolerance because of the inherent physical risk ingesting street drugs, the possibility of brain damage, the loss of educational levels, and lost social development, diminishing a student's ability and chances in life.

Psychologically, the use of drugs and alcohol prohibits the youth from struggling with non-chemical coping skills to solve problems. Typically, sophisticated anger modulation techniques usually learned in late adolescence are missed, leaving the person limited in handling that most important of emotions. Substance abuse is also dangerous, considering the terrible number of automobile crash deaths, teen pregnancies attained while intoxicated, overdose on contaminated substances, and the induction of mental disorders from exposure to harsh substances, such as activation of a latent schizophrenia by use of hallucinogens.

There are three soft signs, less rapacious and life threatening, yet each a debilitating nightmare. They are the three psychosocial declines. The young substance abuser will exhibit losses in functional levels socially and academically previously attained. The adage, "Pot makes a smart kid average and an average kid dumb," is right on the mark. There exist not a few families where pot smoking is a known habit of the parents. The children may start their habit by stealing from the parents. Parental use is hampering national efforts to clean up America, making it almost impossible to convince the child that drugs and alcohol are not good for them,

Social decline can be seen in the youth who are abusing drugs and alcohol. Typically he is one who, if known long enough by educators, will seem to be undergoing a personality change. Characteristically, social withdrawal is first noticed. The student fails to say hello, avoids being near teachers, seems evasive or sneaky, and associates with a lower status group. Obviously, association with known substance abusers is almost always a warning sign. It is unacceptable when told they are just being friends with the known abuser, that they have other kinds of friends too.

There is a sharp demarcation dividing both groups, and usually a young person doesn't straddle the line unless they intend to hop the fence once in a while. The abuser will show up more and more often unclean, unkempt, and disheveled. Actual style of clothes may change to more radical: nose rings, body piercing and tattoo work may follow. Outrageous appearance alone is not a symptom of substance abuse and is used by non-abusing youth, but there does seem to be a high correlation. The socially impaired substance abuser will frequently be late for school, for classes once in school, and other appointments. They seek less and less satisfaction from traditional social functions such as school athletics, rallies, plays, student government, and after school programs. Beware, some abusers use conformity in which to hide, and may be some of the most seriously impaired of all.

Mental and emotional impairment manifests as the disease deepens its grip. Declining academic scores and standardized test scores; loss of interest in school, failure to respond quickly to prompts, sharp noises, or sudden actions, emotional flattening or liability, personality changes, vacant personality, hyperactivity, depression, suicide talk and attempts, psychosis, and a motivation characterize mental and emotional impairments due to substance abuse. Then there are those students, already having emotional problems (about 3-6% of any given population of youth), who are more vulnerable to using drugs and alcohol than well adjusted ones.

Caution is recommended when questioning teenagers who might have another psychiatric illness with which you are unfamiliar. They may present acting as if they are on drugs, but I may be reacting to medications. Or their odd behavior may be due to the psychiatric illness itself, not substance abuse. Knowing a student's history, if available, helps.

Finally comes spiritual decline, an even less obvious manifestation than the previously mentioned signs. By spiritual, the broadest usage is the youth's existential relationship to the greater world around him. Attitudes of respect, humility, wonder and affection indicate a person who has a sense of relationship to something greater at large. Attitudes of contempt, pride, ignorance, and arrogance indicate one who lacks an awareness of the enormity of existence. More specifically, a previously religious or reverent student may suddenly become blatantly disrespectful of organized religion. The inappropriate use of the cross or other religious symbol frequently indicates spiritual decline.

Students are using drugs and alcohol at surprisingly young ages today. Cases exist of ten year old alcoholics. Young people start using drugs and alcohol for one of four reasons:

1) Out of curiosity
2) To party
3) fFom peer pressure
4) To avoid dealing with problems

Intervention is failing today in the last item. Almost every student understands the dangers of drug and alcohol usage. But there are those hard-core users who can't resist involvement because their emotional pain is so high. The causes are many in today's complex world, not the least of which is family and community breakdown.

Today, approximately one-half of families are blended with a similar divorce rate. Children are transported from parent to parent, often against their own wishes. Ex-spouses are not always successful at avoiding retaliating against each other through children. Children from these families feel guilt, anger, and shame, usually unresolved. Once considered relatively harmless to children, divorce is now being re-evaluated as probably the most serious harm of all to children.

Other problems that cause students to have emotional pain include social awkwardness, depression, incipient major mental illnesses, personality disorders, learning disabilities, ADHD, conduct disorder, and substance abuse and dependency in family members. The most common emotional problem found in student populations are parent-child problems, descriptively naming a deficit in communication, authority, and respect between parent and child. A close second is conduct disorder, a behavior set characterized by aggression, exploitation, violence, disregard for the rights of others, animal cruelty, fire setting, bed wetting, defiance, running away, truancy, juvenile arrest record, and associated ADHD, substance abuse, and parent-child problems.

Typically, a student on drugs and/or alcohol will show:
- Lack of muscle coordination
- Wobbly, ataxic gait
- Reddened, puffy eyes (reddened sclera)
- Averted gaze
- Dilated pupils
- Dry eyes
- Dry mouth (anticholinergia)
- Sneezing or sniffing excessively
- Gazing off into space nervousness
- Fine trembling
- Failure to respond to verbal prompts
- Passive-aggressive behavior
- Sudden sickness in class
- Vomiting and chills
- Slurred speech
- Aggression
- Sleep
- Odd, sudden personality changes
- Withdrawal
- An appearance of responding to internal stimuli
- The smell of alcohol or the smell of marijuana (pungent, sharp odor, similar to burning cane)
- The appearance of powder around the nasal opening, on the clothes or hands

Skill 11.2 Identify school and community resources and collaborative procedures to meet the intellectual, personal, and social needs of all students.

Teachers should create personalized learning communities where every student is a valued member and contributor of the classroom experiences. In classrooms where socio-cultural attributes of the student population are incorporated into the fabric of the learning process, dynamic interrelationships are created that enhance the learning experience and the personalization of learning. When students are provided with numerous academic and social opportunities to share cultural incorporations into the learning, everyone in the classroom benefits from bonding through shared experiences and having an expanded viewpoint of a world experience and culture that vastly differs from their own.

In order to create personalized learning communities, educators must use information from the school experience to create relationships that create bridges of collaboration between school and community resources. The interaction chart of personalized learning shows the research of Clarke and Frazer (2003) in evaluating the developmental needs for students in school communities:

Interactions in Personalized Learning

Personal Needs	Relationships	School Practices
Self- Expression	Recognition from school	Provides equity
Creating self-identity	Acceptance-feeling of belonging	Shared community
Choosing one's own path	Creating trust	Range of options for student development
Freedom to take risks	Respect from community	Taking responsibility
Using one's imagination to view self projections	Fulfilling one's purpose in life	Creating greater challenges
Successful mastery	Confirm one's progress and goals	Having clear expectations for performance

(as adapted from Clarke and Frazer, 2003)

In a personalized learning community, students must feel a sense of connection to teachers and staff. Teachers know students by name and individual expression. Greeting students in the morning with names and a special recognition such as, "Jamie, thanks for participating the school's recycling program," or "Great job, David, in that last quarter touchdown at last Friday's football game," will go a long way in creating an affirming and connected school environment.

Researchers continue to show that personalized learning environments increase the learning effect for students; decrease drop-out rates among marginalized students; and decrease unproductive student behavior which can result from constant cultural misunderstandings or miscues between students. Promoting diversity of learning and cultural competency in the classroom for students and teachers creates a world of multicultural opportunities and learning. When students are able to step outside their comfort zones and share themselves, then students grow exponentially in social understanding and cultural connectedness. Examining the world of a homeless student or empathizing with an English Language Learner (ELL) student who has just immigrated to the United States can be important lessons for students to experience.

Personalized learning communities provide supportive learning environments that address the academic and emotional needs of students. As socio-cultural knowledge is conveyed continuously in the interrelated experiences, shared cooperatively, and collaboratively in student groupings or individualized learning, the current and future benefits will continue to present the case and importance of understanding the "whole" child, inclusive of the social and the cultural context.

Students who feel like they belong in their school communities may feel more motivated to succeed academically than students who simply feel like a number among the thousands of students. Parents and community members who are actively involved in PTSAs and community after school support groups will find that students actually appreciate having their support and involvement in school activities and governance.

Community support provides additional resources for classrooms and school communities on limited district budgets. Additional grant sources from local PTSAs and educational organizations continue to provide financial resources for teachers seeking to provide maximal learning opportunities for students.

Skill 11.3 Identify the rights, legal responsibilities, and procedures for reporting incidences of abuse or neglect or other signs of distress.

One of the first things that a teacher learns is how to obtain resources and help for his/her students. All schools have guidelines for receiving this assistance especially since the implementation of the Americans with Disabilities Act. The first step in securing help is for the teacher to approach the school's administration or exceptional education department for direction in attaining special services or resources for qualifying students. Many schools have a committee designated for addressing these needs such as a Child Study Team or Core Team. These teams are made up of both regular and special education teachers, school psychologists, guidance counselors, and administrators. The particular student's classroom teacher usually has to complete some initial paper work and will need to complete some behavioral observations.

The teacher will take this information to the appropriate committee for discussion and consideration. The committee will recommend the next step to be taken. Often subsequent steps include a complete psychological evaluation along with certain physical examinations such as vision and hearing screening and a complete medical examination by a doctor.

The referral of students for this process is usually relatively simple for the classroom teacher and requires little more than some initial paper work and discussion. The services and resources the student receives as a result of the process typically prove to be invaluable to the student with behavioral disorders.

At times, the teacher must go beyond the school system to meet the needs of some students. An awareness of special services and resources and how to obtain them is essential to all teachers and their students. When the school system is unable to address the needs of a student, the teacher often must take the initiative and contact agencies within the community. Frequently there is no special policy for finding resources. It is simply up to the individual teacher to be creative and resourceful and to find whatever help is available to meet the students' needs. Meeting the needs of all students is certainly a team effort that is most often spearheaded by the classroom teacher.

There is a saying, *If you're going to be an alcoholic or drug addict in America, you will be.* Cynical but true, this comment implies exposure to alcohol and drugs is 100%. We now have a wide-spread second generation of drug abusers in families. And alcohol is the oldest for of drug abuse known to humankind, with many families affected for three or more known generations. It's hard to tell youth to eschew drugs when mom and dad, who grew up in the early illicit drug era, have a little toot or smoke and a few drinks on the weekends, or more often.

Educators, therefore, are not only likely to, but often do face students who are high on something in school. Of course, they are not only a hazard to their own safety and those of others, but their ability to be productive learners is greatly diminished, if not non-existent. They show up instead of skip, because it's not always easy or practical for them to spend the day away from home, but not in school. Unless they can stay inside they are at risk of being picked up for truancy. Some enjoy being high in school, getting a sense of satisfaction by putting something over on the system. Some just don't take drug use seriously enough to think usage at school might be inappropriate.

Skill 11.4 Apply knowledge of the contents of, and the procedures for maintaining, permanent student records.

The student permanent record is a file of the student's cumulative educational history. It contains a profile of the student's academic background as well as the student's behavioral and medical background. Other pertinent individual information contained in the permanent record includes the student's attendance, grade averages, and schools attended. Personal information such as parents' names and addresses, immunization records, child's height and weight, and narrative information about the child's progress and physical and mental well being is an important aspect of the permanent record. All information contained within the permanent record is strictly confidential and is only to be discussed with the student's parents or other involved school personnel.

The purpose of the permanent record is to provide applicable information about the student so that the student's individual educational needs can be met. If any specialized testing has been administered, the results are noted in the permanent record. Any special requirements that the student may have are indicated in the permanent record. Highly personal information, including court orders regarding custody, is filed in the permanent record as is appropriate. The importance and value of the permanent record cannot be underestimated. It offers a comprehensive knowledge of the student.

The current teacher is responsible for maintaining the student's permanent record. All substantive information in regard to testing, academic performance, the student's medical condition, and personal events are placed in the permanent record file. Updated information in regard to the student's grades, attendance, and behavior is added annually. These files are kept in a locked fireproof room or file cabinet and cannot be removed from this room unless the person removing them signs a form acknowledging full responsibility for the safe return of the complete file. Again, only the student's parents (or legal guardians), the teacher or other concerned school personnel may view the contents of the permanent record file.

The permanent record file follows the student as he/she moves through the school system with information being added and updated along the way. Anytime the student leaves a school, the permanent record is transferred with the student. The permanent record is regarded as legal documentation of a student's educational experience.

Skill 11.5 Identify the role of teachers on collaborative teams (e.g., IEP, 504, AIP, and child study).

SEE skill 7.5

Skill 11.6 Interpret statewide criterion-referenced assessment data for parents with only rudimentary knowledge of assessment terms and concepts.

The major questions for parents in understanding student performance criterion-referenced data assessment are, "Are students learning?" and "How well are students learning?" Providing parents with a collection of student learning assessment data related to student achievement and performance is a quantifiable response to the questions.

The National Study of School Evaluation (NSSE) 1997 research on School Improvement: Focusing on Student performance adds the following additional questions for parent focus on student learning outcomes:

- What are the types of assessments of student learning that are used in the school?
- What do the results of the data assessments indicate about the current levels of student learning performance? About future predictions? What were the learning objectives and goals?
- What are the strengths and limitations in student learning and achievement?
- How prepared are students for further education or promotion to the next level of education?
- What are the trends seen in student learning in various subject areas or overall academic learning?

At each grade level, the FCAT (Florida Comprehensive Assessment Test) uses the same testing format and scoring for subject areas tested in Reading, Mathematics, Science and Writing. The scale scores range from 100-500 points. Developmental scores noting the annual progress of students are also given with the actual student scores on each section of the testing process. The developmental scores are given from grade to grade level and range from 86 to 3008, so a student taking the test as a 10th grader in 2006 would have a developmental score of 2006. The range of testing scores includes the following:

- High range: 400-500
- Middle range: 325-399
- Low range: 130-324

Students who received scores in the high range in each testing subject area can receive Certificates of Achievement that demonstrate outstanding or notable performances on the Florida Sunshine State Standards. At each grade level of the FCAT, the topic areas are the same, so for example in Science, the tested areas would be:

- Physical and Chemical Science
- Earth and Space Sciences
- Life and Environmental Sciences
- Scientific Thinking

Providing parents with opportunities to attend in-service workshops on data discussions with teachers and administrators creates additional opportunity for parents to ask questions and become actively involved in monitoring their student's educational progress.

With state assessments, parents should look for the words "passed" or "met/exceeded standards" in interpreting the numerical data on student reports. Parents who maintain an active involvement in their students' education will attend school opportunities to promote their understanding of academic and educational achievement for students.

Skill 11.7 Interpret national norm-referenced assessment data for parents with only rudimentary knowledge of assessment terms and concepts.

The Florida Department of Education uses a variety of NRTs to assess student-learning performances. The tests vary in content and assessment knowledge, so they are not interchangeable or comparative between schools and districts. The listing of tests below includes a comprehensive report on the number of students tested and the median national percentile ranking (NPR) of comparative student performance to students in a defined norm group of testers. The NPR is ranked from 1 to 99, where an NPR of 40 means that a student scored the same as or better than 40% of the students testing nationally.

For the parent interpreting NPR assessments, the rule of thumb is that typically 25% of the students test in the lower range of 1-25 and 25% of the students test in the higher range of 76-99, which represents a low and high testing ranking of all test takers nationally. The majority of students test in the range between 26-75.

Florida NRTs (Norm-referenced tests) –1995-1997 Grades 4 & 8
ABBREVIATION TEST

CAT A	California Achievement Test Form A
CAT E/F	California Achievement Test Forms E & F
CTB A/B	Comprehensive Test of Basic Skills Forms A and B
CTB U/V	Comprehensive Test of Basic Skills Forms U and V
ITB K	Iowa Test of Basic Skills Form K
NAT 3	Comprehensive Assessment Program National Achievement Test Form 3
STA E/F	Stanford Achievement Test Forms E and F
STA J/K/L	Stanford Achievement Test Forms J,K & L

(www.floridateachercertifcationtesting.org)

In looking at actual NRT test results from five Florida school districts, parents can see student performance in reading and mathematics in determining trends and predictions of student learning outcomes in school communities. The NRT Grade 8 report for 1997 testing results was taken directly from the Florida Assessment Reports for five school Districts in evaluating student performance in reading and mathematics.

NRT Grade 8 Report - 1997

NORM-REFERENCED TEST REPORT

SPRING 1997

GRADE 8

		READING				MATHEMATICS			
		No. of	Median	Percent in Each NPR Group		No. of	Median	Percent in Each NPR Group	
DISTRICT	TEST	Students	NPR	1-25	76-99	Students	NPR	1-25	76-99
1 ALACHUA	ITB K	1756	54	22	31	1754	54	25	27
2 BAKER	CTB A	248	55	19	28	249	60	18	30
3 BAY	CAT A	1488	56	16	27	1482	60	17	30
4 BRADFORD	CTB A	217	53	25	23	216	46	25	18
5 BREVARD	STA J	3980	57	19	27	3873	58	18	29

(www.floridateachercertifcationtesting.org)

For example in the Alachua District, there were 1,756 students taking the reading tests. Of those students, the median (middle) NPR range was 54% scored in the range from 26-75, with 22% of students testing in the lower range of 1-25, and 31% of students testing in the higher range of 76-99, which typifies the NRT testing results.

Evaluating the math rankings yields comparative ranking results for students for the ITB test. What parents can ascertain is that the results for the Districts 2-5 is that there were a variety of tests given to assess student learning that ranged from the CTB, CAT to the STA norm-reference testing, so the tests cannot be compared to each other because their contents were developed to assess specific student learning outcomes.

Parents must look at the complete student portfolio that includes specific subject area progress reports, discipline records, attendance, and student/teacher logs on in-class performance, and predicted final grade outcome, before making definitive judgments on student learning in school communities. NRT data is only one type of assessment that provides parents with reference information on student academic performance, so parents must reserve judgment until a complete portfolio is obtained from both teachers and students in classrooms.

Competency 12.0   Knowledge of strategies for the implementation of technology in the teaching and learning process.

Skill 12.1 Identify appropriate software to prepare materials, deliver instruction, assess student achievement, and manage classroom tasks.

With a surplus of educational software on the market, it is important for an educator to be able to evaluate a program before purchasing it. Software can vary greatly in content, presentation, skill level, and objectives and it is not always possible to believe everything that is advertised on the package. If a teacher is in the position of having to purchase a computer program for use in the classroom without any prior knowledge of the program itself, it is useful to have some guidelines to follow.   Once a program has been purchased and the shrink-wrap has been removed, many vendors are reluctant to allow its return because of a possible violation of copyright laws or damage to the software medium. For this reason it is important to preview the software personally before buying it. If a vendor is reluctant to allow the teacher to preview a program prior to its purchase, it is sometimes possible to get a preview copy from the publisher.

Many school districts have addressed this problem by publishing a list of approved software titles for each grade level in much the same way that they publish lists of approved text books and other classroom materials. In addition, most districts have developed a software evaluation form to be used by any instructor involved in the purchase of software that is not already on the "approved" list. Use of a software evaluation form can eliminate a lot of the risk involved when shopping for appropriate titles for the classroom. In many districts, all software is evaluated by the actual instructors that will use the software and the completed evaluation forms are made available for the perusal of other prospective buyers.

The first thing that must be considered before purchasing software is its compatibility with the computer on which it is to be used. If the program will not run efficiently on the computer in the classroom because of hardware limitations, there is no need to continue the evaluation process. Some of the restrictions to consider are the operating system (MS-DOS, Windows, or Macintosh) for which the particular software package was developed, the recommended memory size, the required hard drive space, the medium type (floppy disk or CD-ROM), the type of monitor, and the need for any special input devices such as a mouse, joystick, or speech card. If a network is used in the classroom or school for which the program is to be purchased, it is also important to know if the program is able to be used on a network. Often, programs with many graphics encounter difficulties when accessed from a network.

There are three general steps to follow when evaluating a software program. First, one must read the instructions thoroughly to familiarize oneself with the program, its hardware requirements, and its installation. Once the program is installed and ready to run, the evaluator should first run the program as it would be run by a successful student, without deliberate errors but making use of all the possibilities available to the student. Thirdly, the program should be run making deliberate mistakes to test the handling of errors. One should try to make as many different kinds of mistakes as possible, including those for incorrect keyboard usage and the validity of user directions.

Most software evaluation forms include the same types of information. There is usually a section for a general description of the program consisting of the intended grade level, additional support materials available, the type of program (game, simulation, drill, etc), stated goals and objectives, and the clarity of instructions. Other sections will provide checklists for educational content, presentation, and type and quality of user interaction with the program. Once a software package has been thoroughly tested, the teacher will be able to make an intelligent decision regarding its purchase.

When dealing with large class sizes and at the same time trying to offer opportunities for students to use computers, it is often necessary to use ingenuity. If the number of computers available for student use is limited, the teacher must take a tip from elementary school teachers who are skilled at managing centers. Students can be rotated singly or in small groups to the computer centers as long as they are well oriented in advance to the task to be accomplished and with the rules to be observed. Rules for using the computer should be emphasized with the whole class prior to individual computer usage in advance and then prominently posted.

If a computer lab is available for use by the curriculum teacher, the problem of how to give each student the opportunity to use the computer as an educational tool might be alleviated, but a whole new set of problems might occur. Again, the rules to be observed in the computer lab should be discussed before the class ever enters the lab and students should have a thorough understanding of the assignment. When a large group of students is visiting a computer lab, it is very easy for the expensive hardware to suffer from accidental or deliberate harm if the teacher is not aware of what is going on at all times. Students need to be aware of the consequences for not following the rules because it is so tempting to experiment and show off to their peers.

Unfortunately, students who have access to computers outside of school often feel like they know everything already and are reluctant to listen to instruction on lab etiquette or program usage. The teacher must be constantly on guard to prevent physical damage to the machines from foreign objects finding their way into disk drives, key caps from disappearing from keyboards (or being rearranged), or stray pencil or pen marks from appearing on computer systems. Experienced students also get a lot of enjoyment from saving games on hard drives, moving files into new directories or eliminating them altogether, creating passwords to prevent others from using machines, etc.

At the same time other students may need a lot of assistance to prevent accidents caused by their inexperience. It is possible to pair inexperienced students with more capable ones to alleviate some of the problem. Teachers must constantly rotate around the room and students must be prepared before their arrival in the lab so that they know exactly what to do when they get there to prevent them from exercising their creativity.

Skill 12.2 Identify appropriate classroom procedures for student use of available technology.

To a novice, computers might appear to be very complicated machines, but in reality it is not very difficult to operate one of today's user-friendly computers. Basically, all that is required is to attach the computer to the power source and turn it on. Most machines are configured to boot up into a menu of programs from which the user has merely to point and click at the desired choice.

For the computer to boot up from the hard drive follow the instructions for which it has been configured, it is necessary to remove any diskettes from the floppy disk drive before turning on the power. Otherwise, the computer will not boot up into its menu from the hard drive, but rather will try to find the necessary boot up instructions on the floppy disk.

When preparing to shut down the computer, it is important to close all programs that are currently in use. This includes saving anything that needs to be kept for future sessions on the computer. When a program is not properly exited, important data might be lost and the computer might not boot up to the proper menu next time it is turned on. It is just a matter of good housekeeping to put away everything in its proper place before leaving. If the program was accessed from a DOS prompt or menu, the computer should be returned to the same starting place before turning off the machine. Programs accessed from Windows should be exited, all windows should be closed, and Windows itself should be exited by selecting File Exit before the power is turned off. MacIntosh computers are much like Windows in that all programs should be exited and all windows closed before choosing SYSTEM and SHUT DOWN. Once everything is properly closed, the computer will give the user a message ["It is safe to turn off your computer"] and the computer can be turned off.

Skill 12.3 Identify policies and procedures for the safe and ethical use of the Internet, networks, and other electronic media.

Internet usage agreements define a number of criteria for the use of technology that students must agree to in order to have access to school computers. Students must exercise responsibility and accountability in adhering to technology usage during the school day. Students who violate any parts of the computer usage agreement are subject to have all access to school computers or other educational technology denied or blocked, which, for the student needing to print a paper using the school computer and printer, could make the difference in handing assignments in on time or receiving a lower grade for late assignments.

District and school policies are developed to provide a consistent language of expectation for students using school technology. Districts are liable for the actions of students and teachers in school communities who use publicly-funded and legislatively-funded technology. The standards of usage for school computers are created to maximize student use for educational purposes and to minimize student surfing for non-educational sites that minimize learning during class times. The timeframes for computer usage are limited for students, since the numbers of computers being used in school communities are minimal to the users.

Technology use has policies that transcend from the district to school communities to students and staff. Federal and state funding to districts also carry technology expectations as conditions of funding, so the chain of expectation starts from top management to school communities. Given the predator nature of users on the Internet, the policies and procedures for school usage are necessary to keep students safe when they are using computers for educational purposes.

Beyond computer usage in schools, the use of other electronics such as I-pods, walkmans, and cell phones are prohibited in most classrooms. The constant distractions of phones beeping, emitting loud noises, along with the choice of music that each generation listens to on a daily basis impede the educational access for students struggling to maintain focus on the lesson objectives. A student having trouble with inference in a reading passage could be easily distracted with the constant phone noises and electronic music coming from student earphones or computer downloads. An effective teacher underscores in the classroom that the focus on learning will be exclusive of electronic distractions and inappropriate computer use.

Students who have their computer privileges revoked due to abuse of the Internet agreements may find that academic progress may be jeopardized, especially if the students don't own computers or have Internet access beyond the classrooms.

Teachers should monitor the activities of students who are using computers and actively respond to students who misuse public technology intended to enhance the learning process and access for all students.

Skill 12.4 Identify strategies for instructing students in the use of search techniques, the evaluation of data collected, and the preparation of presentations.

The Internet and other research resources provide a wealth of information on thousands of interesting topics for students preparing presentations or projects. Using search engines like Google, Microsoft and Infotrac, student can search multiple Internet resources on one subject search. Students should have an outline of the purpose of a project or research presentation that includes:

- Purpose - Identity the reason for the research information
- Objective - Having a clear thesis for a project will allow the students opportunities to be specific on Internet searches
- Preparation - When using resources or collecting data, students should create folders for sorting through the information. Providing labels for the folders will create a system of organization that will make construction of the final project or presentation easier and less time consuming
- Procedure - Organized folders and a procedural list of what the project or presentation needs to include will create A+ work for students and A+ grading for teachers
- Visuals or artifacts - Choose data or visuals that are specific to the subject content or presentation. Make sure that poster boards or Power Point presentations can be visually seen from all areas of the classroom. Teachers can provide laptop computers for Power Point presentations.

When a teacher models and instructs students in the proper use of search techniques, the teacher can minimize wasted time in preparing projects and wasted paper from students who print every search. In some school districts, students are allowed a minimum number of printed pages per week. Since students have Internet accounts for computer usage, the monitoring of printing is easily done by the school's librarian and teachers in classrooms.

Having the school's librarian or technology expert as a guest speaker in classrooms provides another method of sharing and modeling proper presentation preparation using technology. Teachers can also appoint technology experts from the students in a classroom to work with students on projects and presentations. In high schools, technology classes provide students with upper-class teacher assistants who fill the role of technology assistants.

The wealth of resources for teachers and students seeking to incorporate technology and structured planning for student presentations and projects is as diverse as the presentations. There is an expert in every classroom who is always willing to offer advice and instruction. In school communities, that expert may begin with the teacher.

Many school districts have shared drives that contain multiple files of lesson and unit plans, curriculum maps, pacing guides, and assessment ideas. While these can be very beneficial, it is always a good idea to determine the intended use for such files and documents.

Competency 13.0   Knowledge of the history of education and its philosophical and sociological foundations.

Skill 13.1 Apply historical, philosophical, and sociological perspectives to contemporary issues in American education.

To understand where we are today in American public education is to appreciate how politics, history, research, society, and the economy have all come together to develop a complex, sometimes bureaucratic, system of teaching and learning.

Debates on instruction have typically focused on the role of the teacher. Some people argue that child-centered instruction is favorable, as it is more engaging for students. Others have advocated for more traditional methods, such as lecturing, note-taking, and other teacher-centered activities.

Historically, public education has evolved from being something relegated to the wealthy. Education was usually private, tutor-based, and uneven. The concept of a free public education was developed in order to ensure that as many people in this country could participate in (and further develop) the nation's economy. Decades ago, a small one-room schoolhouse sufficed, but today, each neighborhood requires multiple schools to educate all of the local children. In these traditional settings, the teacher was the lecturer and leader of all instruction.

As the population has grown, the structure of public schooling has been shaped by bureaucracy. To accommodate all the children, the structures of public schools have changed so each child would have a similar, equal education no matter which school s/he attended. As classrooms and research grew more beneficial instructional styles emerged, many classroom teachers began to incorporate cooperative learning, learning centers, reading and writing workshops, group projects (and other developmentally appropriate styles) into their classroom.

Another huge change in schools has been governance. Governance refers to how schools are run. Even though schools are still technically run by local, elected school boards, the federal government is increasingly taking a role in public education. It used to be that schools would have to answer to no higher authority than states. Now, with *No Child Left Behind*, the federal government has taken a greater role in how schools are run.

Another issue in governance has been the debate between local, neighborhood schools and choice schools. Neighborhood schools are those in which students attend based on home address. For the past few decades, some school districts have provided students with the option of attending magnet schools, or schools that are available for any student within the district.

Usually, these schools have themes, such as business academies or college preparatory curricula. In addition to magnet schools, money now is available for charter schools that do not have to abide by the same policies as regular public schools. Magnet schools do not have to be run by school districts, but they take money from the districts in which their students originate. So, for example, if the local public school gets $5000 per student per school year from local property taxes and the state (or however the state finances schools), that $5000 would instead go to the charter school if one student opted to go there.

Finally, in some states and cities, voucher money is available for students attending private schools. This is where the government gives parents part or all of the money that would have been put into the local public district(s) so that they can use it to send their children to private schools. None of these options above is without controversy in this country.

Philosophically, most of the debate that has shaped public education has focused on curriculum, instruction, and assessment. For example, standards-based education is a curricular move to ensure that all students from a state learn the same knowledge. Debate has centered on three ideas: first, that some knowledge is not developmentally appropriate; second, that the standards are not appropriate for all students; third, that most states' standards are too thick, causing teachers to have to teach too much in a school year (and therefore, not allowing teachers to go into depth with particular topics that may be of interest to students).

Debates on instruction have focused on the role of the teacher. Some people argue that child-centered instruction is favorable, as it is more engaging for students. Others have advocated for more traditional methods, such as lecturing, note-taking, and other teacher-centered activities.

Debates on assessment have focused on the role of testing students, as well as the appropriateness of testing them for school evaluation purposes. First, most state tests take hours to complete, and many teachers argue that it wastes instructional time. Others argue that state tests do not assess what is really taught in schools.

Such people suggest that performance assessments would be more appropriate. Performance assessments evaluate students' ability to do tasks related to their learning. For example, a performance assessment in Language Arts could be a timed essay. Students would have to write an essay in a specific amount of time, and possibly, the teacher would score it with a rubric or scoring guide. Grading students, in general, has been an important topic. There are those out there who advocate eliminating letter grades; some school districts have even started to grade students not by subject, but by standard (from state standards).

Sociologically, schools have faced many unique challenges. As schools are charged with educating all students within the neighborhood, changes in demographics and economics have impacted schools. While laws have been set up to eliminate segregation in schools, many inner-city children attend highly segregated schools based on the demographic compositions of their neighborhoods. For some time, districts instituted bussing policies to combat this. This is where a student in one neighborhood might be put on a bus and sent to a school in another neighborhood with a different ethnic or racial mixture. Many districts did find that this was impractical, as it caused some students to have to spend hours per day on busses when they could have been doing other more productive things.

Many districts around the country are just learning how to deal with larger immigrant populations as more immigrants leave the historically popular entry points, such as Texas and California. Those districts must learn how to develop appropriate English language programs to assist their children in learning English; they must also learn to work with parents who may be scared about involvement with schools.

Skill 13.2 Identify contemporary philosophical views on education that influence teaching.

Today, teachers are immediately faced with the challenge of deciding whether they believe that the classroom should be run as teacher-centered or student-centered. While the most probable answer is that an appropriate combination of both is preferred, most teachers must negotiate which areas of their instruction should be teacher-centered and which areas should be student-centered.

Teacher-centered classrooms generally focus on the concept that knowledge is objective and that students must learn new information through the transmission of that knowledge from the teacher. Student-centered classrooms are considered to be constructivist, in that students are given opportunities to construct their own meanings to new pieces of knowledge. Doing so may require that students are more actively involved in the learning process. Indeed, constructivism is a strong force in teaching today, but it does get misinterpreted a lot. Good constructivist teachers do NOT just let their students explore anything they want in any way they choose; rather they give students opportunities to learn things in more natural ways, such as experiments, hands-on projects, discussion, etc.

For quite some time, a movement called multiple intelligences was popular in many classrooms. This theory suggested that there are at least seven different types of intelligence, and that verbal and quantitative intelligences, the two types that are most often associated with intellect, should be re-considered as less important as they once were. Other intelligences included kinesthetic, inter-personal, musical, intra-personal, and spatial. This theory helped teachers understand that while some students may not be expert in one style of learning, it is entirely possible that they are incredibly gifted in another.

Various subject areas have added to philosophical debates of teaching. For example, reading teachers have long debated whether phonics or whole language was more appropriate as an instructional methodology. Language Arts teachers have debated the importance of the canon (famous works of literature); some teachers feel that the canon is irrelevant and that the only reason to teach literature is to teach thinking skills and an appreciation of good literature. Math teachers have debated the extent to which application is necessary in math instruction; some feel that it is more important to teach structure and process, while others feel it is only important to teach math skills in context.

Competency 14.0   Knowledge of specific approaches, methods, and strategies appropriate for students with limited English proficiency.

Skill 14.1 Identify characteristics of first and second language acquisition.

One of the most important things to know about the differences between L1 (first language) and L2 (second language) acquisition is that people usually will master L1, but they will almost never be fully proficient in L2. However, if children can be trained in L2 before about the age of seven, their chances at full mastery will be much higher.

Children learn language with little effort, which is why they can be babbling at one year and speaking with complete, complex ideas just a few years later. It is important to know that language is innate, meaning that our brains are ready to learn a language from birth. Yet a lot of language learning is behavioral, meaning that children imitate adults' speech.

L2 acquisition is much harder for adults. Multiple theories of L2 acquisition have come developed. One of the more notable ones come from Jim Cummins. Cummins argues that there are two types of language that usually need to be acquired by students learning English as a second language: Basic Interpersonal Communication Skills (BICS) Cognitive Academic Language Proficiency (CALP).

BICS is general, everyday language used to communicate simple thoughts, whereas CALP is the more complex, academic language used in school. It is harder for students to acquire CALP, and many teachers mistakenly assume that students can learn complex academic concepts in English if they have already mastered BICS. The truth is that CALP takes much longer to master, and in some cases, particularly with little exposure in certain subjects, it may never be mastered.

Another set of theories is based on Stephen Krashen's research in L2 acquisition. Most people understand his theories based on five principles:

1. The acquisition-learning hypothesis: This states that there is a difference between learning a language and acquiring it. Children "acquire" a first language easily—it's natural. But adults often have to "learn" a language through coursework, studying, and memorizing. One can acquire a second language, but often it requires more deliberate and natural interaction within that language.

2. <u>The monitor hypothesis</u>: This is when the learned language "monitors" the acquired language. In other words, this is when a person's "grammar check" kicks in and keeps awkward, incorrect language out of a person's L2 communication.
3. <u>The natural order hypothesis</u>: This suggests that the learning of grammatical structures is predictable and follows a "natural order."
4. <u>The input hypothesis</u>: Some people call this "comprehensible input." This means that a language learner will learn best when the instruction or conversation is just above the learner's ability. That way, the learner has the foundation to understand most of the language, but still will have to figure out, often in context, what that extra more difficult element means.
5. <u>The affective filter hypothesis</u>: This suggests that people will learn a second language when they are relaxed, have high levels of motivation, and have a decent level of self-confidence.

ESOL students may need additional accommodations with assessments, assignments, and projects. For example, teachers may find that written tests provide little to no information about a student's understanding of the content. Therefore, an oral test may be better suited for ESOL students. When students are somewhat comfortable and capable with written tests, a shortened test may actually be preferable; take note that they will need extra time to translate.

Skill 14.2 Identify ESOL approaches, methods, and strategies (e.g., materials adaptation, alternative assessment, and strategy documentation) appropriate for instruction.

Teaching students who are learning English as a second language poses some unique challenges, particularly in a standards-based environment. The key is realizing that no matter how little English a student knows, the teacher should teach with the student's developmental level in mind. This means that instruction should not be "dumbed-down" for ESOL students. Different approaches should be used, however, to ensure that these students (a) get multiple opportunities to learn and practice English and (b) still learn content.

Many ESOL approaches are based on social learning methods. By being placed in mixed level groups or by being paired with a student of another ability level, students will get a chance to practice English in a natural, non-threatening environment. Students should not be pushed in these groups to use complex language or to experiment with words that are too difficult. They should simply get a chance to practice with simple words and phrases.

In teacher-directed instructional situations, visual aids, such as pictures, objects, and video are particularly effective at helping students make connections between words and items with which they are already familiar.

Skill 14.3 Identify and apply cognitive approaches, multisensory ESOL strategies, and instructional practices that build upon students' abilities and promote self-worth.

From high school and college, most of us think that learning a language strictly involves drills, memorization, and tests. While this is a common method used (some people call it a structural, grammatical, or linguistic approach). While this works for some students, it certainly does not work for all.

Although there are dozens of methods that have been developed to help people learn additional languages, these are on some of the more common approaches used in today's K-12 classrooms. Cognitive approaches to language learning focus on concepts. While words and grammar are important, when teachers use the cognitive approach, they focus on using language for conceptual purposes— rather than learning words and grammar for the sake of simply learning new words and grammatical structures. This approach focuses heavily on students' learning styles, and it cannot necessarily be pinned down as having specific techniques. Rather, it is more of a philosophy of instruction.

There are many approaches that are noted for their motivational purposes. In a general sense, when teachers work to motivate students to learn a language, they do things to help reduce fear and to assist students in identifying with native speakers of the target language. A very common method is often called the functional approach. In this approach, the teacher focuses on communicative elements. For example, a first grade English as a Second Language (ESOL) teacher might help students learn phrases that will assist them in finding a restroom, asking for help on the playground, etc. Many functionally-based adult ESOL programs help learners with travel-related phrases and words.

Another very common motivational approach is Total Physical Response. This is a kinesthetic approach that combines language learning and physical movement. In essence, students learn new vocabulary and grammar by responding with physical motion to verbal commands. Some people say it is particularly effective because the physical actions help to create good brain connections with the words.

In general, the best methods do not treat students as if they have a language deficit. Rather, the best methods build upon what students already know, and they help to instill the target language as a communicative process rather than a list of vocabulary words that have to be memorized.

In addition to these methods, it is important that, particularly when second language learners have multiple teachers, such as in middle or high school, that teachers communicate and collaborate in order to provide a great level consistency. It is particularly difficult for second language learners to go from one class to the next, where there are different sets of expectations and varied methods of instruction, and still focus on the more complex elements of learning language.

When students have higher levels of anxiety regarding the learning of a second language, they will be less likely to focus on the language; rather, they will be focusing on whatever it is that is creating their anxiety. This does not mean that standards and expectations should be different for these students in all classes; it simply means that teachers should have common expectations so that students know what to expect in each class and don't have to think about the differences between classes.

Another hugely important reason for teachers to collaborate, particularly with the ESOL specialists, is to ensure that students are showing consistent development across classes. Where there is inconsistency, teachers should work to uncover what it is that is keeping the student from excelling in a particular class.

The most important concept to remember regarding the difference between learning a first language and a second one is that if the learner is approximately age seven or older, learning a second language will occur very differently in the learner's brain than it will had the learner been younger.

The reason for this is that there is a language-learning function that exists in young children that appears to go away as they mature. Learning a language prior to age seven is almost guaranteed, with relatively little effort. The mind is like a sponge, and it soaks up language very readily. Some theorists, including the famous linguist Noam Chomsky, argue that the brain has a "universal grammar" and that only vocabulary and very particular grammatical structures, related to specific languages, need to be introduced in order for a child to learn a language. What this really means is that, in essence, there are slots into which language gets filled in a child's mind. This is definitely not the case with learning a second language after about seven years old.

Learning a second language as a pre-adolescent, adolescent, or adult requires quite a bit of translation from the first language to the second. Vocabulary and grammar particulars are memorized, not necessarily internalized (at least, as readily as a first language). In fact, many (though not all) people who are immersed in a second language never fully function as fluent in the language. They may appear to be totally fluent, but often there will be small traits that are hard to pick up and internalize.

It is fairly clear that learning a second language successfully does require fluency in the first language. This is because, as stated above, the second language is translated from the first in the learner's mind. First language literacy is also a crucial factor in second language learning, particularly second language literacy.

When helping second language learners make the "cross-over" in language fluency or literacy from first language to second language, it is important to help them identify strategies they use in the first language and apply those to the second language. It is also important to note similarities and differences in phonetic principals in the two languages. Sometimes it is helpful to encourage students to translate; other times, it is helpful for them to practice production in the target language. In either case, teachers must realize that learning a second language is a slow and complicated process.

Sample Test

1. **What would improve planning for instruction?**
   (Skill 1.1, Average Rigor)

   A. Describe the role of the teacher and student

   B. Evaluate the outcomes of instruction

   C. Rearrange the order of activities

   D. Give outside assignments

2. **What is the best definition for an achievement test?**
   (Skill 1.1, Rigorous)

   A. It measures mechanical and practical abilities

   B. It measures broad areas of knowledge that are the result of cumulative learning experiences

   C. It measures the ability to learn to perform a task

   D. It measures performance related to specific, recently acquired information

3. **Norm-referenced tests:**
   (Skill 1.1, Rigorous)

   A. Give information only about the local samples results.

   B. Provide information about how the local test takers did compared to a representative sampling of national test takers.

   C. Make no comparisons to national test takers.

   D. None of the above.

4. **A standardized test will be:**
   (Skill 1.1, Easy)

   A. Given out with the same predetermined questions and format to all.

   B. Not be given to certain children.

   C. If given out in exactly the same format with the same content, may be taken over a lengthier test period (i.e. 4 hours instead of three or two).

   D. All of the above.

5. Which of the following describes why it is important and necessary for teachers to be able to analyze data on their students?
(Skill 1.2, Rigorous)

   A. To provide appropriate instruction

   B. To make instructional decisions

   C. To communicate and determine instructional progress

   D. All of the above

6. How are standardized tests useful in assessment?
(Skill 1.2, Average Rigor)

   A. For teacher evaluation

   B. For evaluation of the administration

   C. For comparison from school to school

   D. For comparison to the population on which the test was normed

7. What is evaluation of the instructional activity based on?
(Skill 1.3, Average Rigor)

   A. Student grades

   B. Teacher evaluation

   C. Student participation

   D. Specified criteria

8. What must be a consideration when a parent complains that he/she can't control their child's behavior?
(Skill 1.3, Average Rigor)

   A. Consider whether the parent gives feedback to the child

   B. Consider whether the parent's expectations for control are developmentally appropriate

   C. Consider how much time the parent spends with the child

   D. Consider how rigid the rules are that the parent sets

9. If teachers attend to content, instructional materials, activities, learner needs, and goals in instructional planning, what could be an outcome?
(Skill 1.3, Rigorous)

A. Planning for the next year

B. Effective classroom performance

C. Elevated test scores on standardized tests

D. More student involvement

10. Mrs. Grant is providing her students with many extrinsic motivators in order to increase their intrinsic motivation. Which of the best explains this relationship?
(Skill 1.4, Rigorous)

A. This is a good relationship and will increase intrinsic motivation

B. The relationship builds animosity between the teacher and the students

C. Extrinsic motivation does not in itself help to build intrinsic motivation

D. There is no place for extrinsic motivation in the classroom

11. Which of the following is considered a study skill?
(Skill 1.4, Easy)

A. Using graphs, tables, and maps

B. Using a desk-top publishing program

C. Explaining important vocabulary words

D. Asking for clarification

12. Which of the following test items is not objective?
(Skill 1.4, Easy)

A. Multiple choice

B. Essay

C. Matching

D. True/false

13. What should a teacher do when students have not responded well to an instructional activity?
(Skill 2.1, Rigorous)

A. Reevaluate learner needs

B. Request administrative help

C. Continue with the activity another day

D. Assign homework on the concept

14. **Why is it important for a teacher to pose a question before calling on students to answer?**
(Skill 2.1, Average Rigor)

A. It helps manage student conduct

B. It keeps the students as a group focused on the class work

C. It allows students time to collaborate

D. It gives the teacher time to walk among the students

15. **Which statement is an example of specific praise?**
(Skill 2.1, Average Rigor)

A. "John, you are the only person in class not paying attention"

B. "William, I thought we agreed that you would turn in all of your homework"

C. "Robert, you did a good job staying in line. See how it helped us get to music class on time"

D. "Class, you did a great job cleaning up the art room"

16. **What is one way a teacher can supplement verbal praise?**
(Skill 2.1, Easy)

A. Help students evaluate their own performance and supply self-reinforcement

B. Give verbal praise more frequently

C. Give tangible rewards such as stickers or treats

D. Have students practice giving verbal praise

17. **The teacher states that students will review the material from the previous day, demonstrate an electronic circuit, and set up an electronic circuit in small groups. What has the teacher demonstrated?**
(Skill 2.1, Average Rigor)

A. The importance of reviewing

B. Giving the general framework for the lesson to facilitate learning

C. Giving students the opportunity to leave if they are not interested in the lesson

D. Providing momentum for the lesson

18. What is one benefit of amplifying a student's response?
(Skill 2.1, Average Rigor)

A. It helps the student develop a positive self-image

B. It is helpful to other students who are in the process of learning the reasoning or steps in answering the question

C. It allows the teacher to cover more content

D. It helps to keep the information organized

19. When is optimal benefit reached when handling an incorrect student response?
(Skill 2.1, Rigorous)

A. When specific praise is used

B. When the other students are allowed to correct that student

C. When the student is redirected to a better problem solving approach

D. When the teacher asks simple questions, provides cues to clarify, or gives assistance for working out the correct response

20. How can the teacher help students become more work oriented and less disruptive?
(Skill 2.1, Average Rigor)

A. Seek their input for content instruction

B. Challenge the students with a task and show genuine enthusiasm for it

C. Use behavior modification techniques with all students

D. Make sure lesson plans are complete for the week

21. What has been established to increase student originality, intrinsic motivation, and higher order thinking skills?
(Skill 2.1, Rigorous)

A. Classroom climate

B. High expectations

C. Student choice

D. Use of authentic learning opportunities

22. What is an example of formative feedback?
(Skill 2.1, Easy)

A. The results of an intelligence test

B. Correcting the tests in small groups

C. Verbal behavior that expresses approval of a student response to a test item

D. Scheduling a discussion prior to the test

23. Why is it important for the teacher to alert non-performers when conducting activities?
(Skill 2.1, Rigorous)

A. It creates suspense

B. Students will take over the discipline

C. Students will become more work involved

D. Students will more likely not take part in the recitation

24. Mrs. Shapiro states, "During the past four weeks we have discussed national and international conditions which led to the outbreak of World War II. Tomorrow we are going to spend some time going over them again and comparing and contrasting them with conditions in the world today. Make a list of these conditions from your class notes, and let's see how complete our lists are." What is this an example of?
(Skill 2.1, Rigorous)

A. Topic summary within the lesson

B. Weekly summary and recap

C. Lesson-end review

D. Test preparation

25. Ms. Smith says, "Yes, exactly what do you mean by "It was the author's intention to mislead you." What does this illustrate?
(Skill 2.1, Rigorous)

A. Digression

B. Restates response

C. Probes a response

D. Amplifies a response

26. What is a frequently used type of feedback to students?
(Skill 2.1, Rigorous)

A. Correctives

B. Simple praise-confirmation

C. Correcting the response

D. Explanations

27. What can be concluded from research on concept teaching?
(Skill 2.1, Average Rigor)

A. The most effective way is oral presentation and visual examples

B. The most effective way is to use manipulatives and oral presentation

C. The most effective way is to use a definition with examples and non-examples

D. The most effective way is to use visuals and manipulatives

28. What is the definition of a non-performer?
(Skill 2.1, Rigorous)

A. Students who are off-task

B. Students not chosen to answer a teacher-posed question

C. Students with stanine scores of 20 or below

D. Students who consistently score below 50 percent on classroom tests

29. What is not a way that teachers show acceptance and give value to a student response?
(Skill 2.1, Rigorous)

A. Acknowledging

B. Correcting

C. Discussing

D. Amplifying

30. What is teacher with-it-ness?
(Skill 2.1, Rigorous)

A. Having adequate knowledge of subject matter

B. A skill that must be mastered to attain certification

C. Understanding the current fads and trends that affect students

D. Attending to two tasks at once

31. The teacher responds, "Yes, that is correct" to a student's answer. What is this an example of?
(Skill 2.1, Rigorous)

A. Academic feedback

B. Academic praise

C. Simple positive response

D. Simple negative response

32. Which of the following is not a characteristic of effective praise?
(Skill 2.1, Average Rigor)

A. Praise is delivered in front of the class so it will serve to motivate others

B. Praise is low-key

C. Praise provides information about student competence

D. Praise is delivered contingently

33. What are teacher redirects?
(Skill 2.1, Average Rigor)

A. The teacher redirects the deviant behavior to another task

B. The teacher changes the focus of the class to provide smooth transitions

C. The teacher changes student jobs every nine weeks

D. The teacher asks a second student to expound on the first student's answer

34. Discovery learning is to inquiry as direct instruction is to...
(Skill 2.3, Rigorous)

A. Scripted lessons

B. Well-developed instructions

C. Clear instructions which eliminate all misinterpretations

D. Creativity of teaching

35. The concept of efficient use of time includes which of the following?
(Skill 2.3, Rigorous)

A. Daily review, seatwork, and recitation of concepts

B. Lesson initiation, transition, and comprehension check

C. Review, test, review

D. Punctuality, management transition, and wait time avoidance

36. The success oriented classroom is designed to ensure students are successful at attaining new skills. In addition, mistakes are viewed as… in this type of classroom.
(Skill 2.3, Rigorous)

A. Motivations to improve

B. Natural part of the learning process

C. Ways to improve

D. Building blocks

37. Which of the following can impact the desire of students to learn new material?
(Skill 2.3, Easy)

A. Assessments plan

B. Lesson plans

C. Enthusiasm

D. School community

38. How can mnemonic devices be used to increase achievement?
(Skill 2.3, Average Rigor)

A. They help the child rehearse the information

B. They help the child visually imagine the information

C. They help the child to code information

D. They help the child reinforce concepts

39. What is the definition of proactive classroom management?
(Skill 2.3, Rigorous)

A. Management that is constantly changing

B. Management that is downplayed

C. Management that gives clear and explicit instructions and rewarding compliance

D. Management that is designed by the students

40. What is the most significant development emerging in children at age two?
(Skill 2.4, Average Rigor)

A. Immune system develops

B. Socialization occurs

C. Language develops

D. Perception develops

41. When communicating with parents for whom English is not the primary language you should:
(Skill 2.4, Easy)

A. Provide materials whenever possible in their native language

B. Use an interpreter

C. Provide the same communication as you would to native English speaking parents

D. All of the above

42. What has research shown to be the effect of using advance organizers in the lesson?
(Skill 2.4, Average Rigor)

A. They facilitate learning and retention

B. They enhance retention only

C. They only serve to help the teacher organize the lesson

D. They show definitive positive results on student achievement

43. When developing lessons it is imperative teachers provide equity in pedagogy so…
(Skill 3.1, Rigorous)

A. Unfair labeling of students will occur

B. Student experiences will be positive

C. Students will achieve academic success

D. All of the above

44. What is a benefit of frequent self-assessment?
(Skill 3.1, Easy)

A. Opens new venues for professional development

B. Saves teachers the pressure of being observed by others

C. Reduces time spent on areas not needing attention

D. Offers a model for students to adopt in self-improvement

45. Mrs. Graham has taken the time to reflect, complete observations, and asked for feedback about the interactions between her and her students from her principal. It is obvious by seeking this information out that Mrs. Graham understands which of the following?
(Skill 3.2, Rigorous)

A. The importance of clear communication with the principal

B. She needs to analyze her effectiveness of classroom interactions

C. She is clearly communicating with the principal

D. She cares about her students

46. Which of the following is a good reason to collaborate with a peer:
(Skill 3.2, Easy)

A. To increase your knowledge in areas where you feel you are weak, but the peer is strong

B. To increase your planning time and that of your peer by combining the classes and taking more breaks

C. To have fewer lesson plans to write

D. To teach fewer subjects

47. Which of the following are ways a professional can assess his/her teaching strengths and weaknesses? (Skill 3.2, Rigorous)

A. Examining how many students were unable to understand a concept

B. Asking peers for suggestions or ideas

C. Self-evaluation/Reflection of lessons taught

D. All of the above

48. What would improve planning for instruction? (Skill 4.1, Average Rigor)

A. Describe the role of the teacher and student

B. Evaluate the outcomes of instruction

C. Rearrange the order of activities

D. Give outside assignments

49. Which of the following type of question will not stimulate higher-level critical thinking?

(Skill 4.1 Rigorous)

A. A hypothetical question

B. An open-ended question

C. A close-ended question

D. A judgment question

50. Which of the following is <u>not</u> one of the levels of Bloom's taxonomy? (Skill 4.1, Average Rigor)

A. Synthesis

B. Evaluation

C. Understanding

D. Knowledge

51. Mr. Ryan has proposed to his classroom that the students may demonstrate understanding of the unit taught in a variety of ways including: taking a test, writing a paper, creating an oral presentation, or building a model/project. Which of the following areas of differentiation has Mr. Ryan demonstrated?
(Skill 4.1, Rigorous)

A. Synthesis

B. Product

C. Content

D. Product

52. What is an example of a low order question?
(Skill 4.1, Average Rigor)

A. "Why is it important to recycle items in your home?"

B. "Compare how glass and plastics are recycled."

C. "What items do we recycle in our county?"

D. "Explain the importance of recycling in our county.

53. Which of the following is an example of a synthesis question according to Bloom's taxonomy?
(Skill 4.1, Rigorous)

A. "What is the definition of_____?"

B. "Compare ____ to ____."

C. "Match column A to column B."

D. "Propose an alternative to_____."

54. When is content teaching effective?
(Skill 4.1, Average Rigor)

A. When it is presented in demonstration form

B. When the teacher separates the content into distinct elements

C. When the content is covered over a long span of time

D. When the decision about content is made at the district level

55. Wait-time has what effect? (Skill 4.2, Average Rigor)

A. Gives structure to the class discourse

B. Fewer chain and low level questions are asked with more higher level questions included

C. Gives the students time to evaluate the response

D. Gives the opportunity for in-depth discussion about the topic

56. What is an effective amount of "wait time"? (Skill 4.2, Rigorous)

A. 1 second

B. 5 seconds

C. 15 seconds

D. 10 seconds

57. How can the teacher establish a positive climate in the classroom? (Skill 5.1, Average Rigor)

A. Help students see the unique contributions of individual differences

B. Use whole group instruction for all content areas

C. Help students divide into cooperative groups based on ability

D. Eliminate teaching strategies that allow students to make choices

58. What do cooperative learning methods all have in common? (Skill 5.1, Average Rigor)

A. Philosophy

B. Cooperative task/cooperative reward structures

C. Student roles and communication

D. Teacher roles

59. What is a good strategy for teaching ethnically diverse students?
(Skill 5.2, Average Rigor)

A. Don't focus on the students' culture

B. Expect them to assimilate easily into your classroom

C. Imitate their speech patterns

D. Include ethnic studies in the curriculum

60. Which of the following is an example of a restriction within the affective domain?
(Skill 5.2, Easy)

A. Unable to think abstractly

B. Inability to synthesize information

C. Inability to concentrate

D. Inability complete physical activities

61. What developmental patterns should a professional teacher assess to meet the needs of the student?
(Skill 6.1, Rigorous)

A. Academic, regional, and family background

B. Social, physical, academic

C. Academic, physical, and family background

D. Physical, family, ethnic background

62. Which is true of child protective services?
(Skill 6.2, Average Rigor)

A. They have been forced to become more punitive in their attempts to treat and prevent child abuse and neglect

B. They have become more a means for identifying cases of abuse and less an agent for rehabilitation due to the large volume of cases

C. They have become advocates for structured discipline within the school

D. They have become a strong advocate in the court system

63. Students who can solve problems mentally have…
(Skill 7.1, Average Rigor)

A. Reached maturity

B. Physically developed

C. Reached the pre-operational stage of thought

D. Achieved the ability to manipulate objects symbolically

64. Mrs. Potts has noticed an undercurrent in her classroom of an unsettled nature. She is in the middle of her math lesson, but still notices that many of her students seem to be having some sort of difficulty. Mrs. Potts stops class and decides to have a class meeting. She understands that even though her math objectives are important, it is equally important to address whatever is troubling her classroom. What is it Mrs. Potts knows? (Skill 7.1, Rigorous)

A. Discipline is important

B. Social issues can impact academic learning

C. Maintaining order is important

D. Social skills instruction is important

65. In successful inclusion of students with disabilities: (Skill 7.1, Average Rigor)

A. A variety of instructional arrangements are available

B. School personnel shift the responsibility for learning outcomes to the student

C. The physical facilities are used as they are

D. Regular classroom teachers have sole responsibility for evaluating student progress

66. Which of the following is not a communication issue that is related to diversity within the classroom? (Skill 7.2, Average Rigor)

A. Learning disorder

B. Sensitive terminology

C. Body language

D. Discussing differing viewpoints and opinions

67. When are students more likely to understand complex ideas? (Skill 7.3, Rigorous)

A. If they do outside research before coming to class

B. Later when they write out the definitions of complex words

C. When they attend a lecture on the subject

D. When they are clearly defined by the teacher and are given examples and nonexamples of the concept

68. What have recent studies regarding effective teachers concluded? (Skill 7.3, Rigorous)

A. Effective teachers let students establish rules

B. Effective teachers establish routines by the sixth week of school

C. Effective teachers state their own policies and establish consistent class rules and procedures on the first day of class

D. Effective teachers establish flexible routines

69. When is utilization of instructional materials most effective? (Skill 7.3, Average Rigor)

A. When the activities are sequenced

B. When the materials are prepared ahead of time

C. When the students choose the pages to work on

D. When the students create the instructional materials

70. If teachers attend to content, instructional materials, activities, learner needs, and goals in instructional planning, what could be an outcome? (Skill 7.3, Rigorous)

A. Planning for the next year

B. Effective classroom performance

C. Elevated test scores on standardized tests

D. More student involvement

71. When creating and selecting materials for instruction, teachers should complete which of the following steps:
(Skill 7.3, Average Rigor)

A. Relevant to the prior knowledge of the students

B. Allow for a variation of learning styles

C. Choose alternative teaching strategies

D. All of the above

72. The teacher states, "We will work on the first page of vocabulary words. On the second page we will work on the structure and meaning of the words. We will go over these together and then you will write out the answers to the exercises on your own. I will be circulating to give help if needed". What is this an example of?
(Skill 7.3, Rigorous)

A. Evaluation of instructional activity

B. Analysis of instructional activity

C. Identification of expected outcomes

D. Pacing of instructional activity

73. According to Piaget, what stage is characterized by the ability to think abstractly and to use logic?
(Skill 7.4, Easy)

A. Concrete operations

B. Pre-operational

C. Formal operations

D. Conservative operational

74. At approximately what age is the average child able to define abstract terms such as honesty and justice? (Skill 7.4, Rigorous)

A. 10-12 years old

B. 4-6 years old

C. 14-16 years old

D. 6-8 years old

75. According to Piaget's theory of cognitive development, what is the process of incorporating new objects, information or experiences into the existing cognitive structures?
(Skill 7.4, Average Rigor)

A. Attachment

B. Conservation

C. Identification

D. Assimilation

76. Which of following is <u>not</u> the role of the teacher in the instructional process:
(Skill 7.4, Average Rigor)

A. Instructor

B. Coach

C. Facilitator

D. Follower

77. How many stages of intellectual development does Piaget define?
(Skill 7.4, Easy)

A. Two

B. Four

C. Six

D. Eight

78. When using a kinesthetic approach, what would be an appropriate activity?
(Skill 7.4, Easy)

A. List

B. Match

C. Define

D. Debate

79. Who developed the theory of multiple intelligences?
(Skill 7.4, Easy)

A. Bruner

B. Gardner

C. Kagan

D. Cooper

80. Piaget's learning theory asserts that adolescents in the formal operations period...
(Skill 7.4 , Rigorous)

A. Behave properly from fear of punishment rather than from a conscious decision to take a certain action.

B. See the past more realistically and can relate to people from the past more than preadolescents.

C. Are less self-conscious and thus more willing to project their own identities into those of fictional characters.

D. Have not yet developed a symbolic imagination.

81. According to Piaget, what is a child born with?
(Skill 7.4, Rigorous)

   A. The tendency to actively relate pieces of information acquired

   B. The ability to adapt

   C. Primary emotions

   D. Desire

82. Which of the following is a presentation modification?
(Skill 7.5, Easy)

   A. Taking an assessment in an alternate room

   B. Providing an interpreter to give the test in American Sign Language

   C. Allowing dictation of written responses

   D. Extending the time limits on an assessment

83. According to Piaget, when does the development of symbolic functioning and language take place?
(Skill 7.4, Average Rigor)

   A. Concrete operations stage

   B. Formal operations stage

   C. Sensorimotor stage

   D. Preoperational stage

84. What would the presence of a low attention span and restlessness in a child be a possible indication of?
(Skill 7.5, Rigorous)

   A. Anger

   B. Retardation

   C. Hyperkinesis

   D. Adaptation

85. The major difference between phonemic and phonological awareness is:
(Skill 8.1, Easy)

   A. One deals with a series of discrete sounds and the other with sound-spelling relationships.

   B. One is involved with teaching and learning alliteration and rhymes.

   C. Phonemic awareness is a specific type of phonological awareness that deals with separate phonemes within a given word.

   D. Phonological awareness is associated with printed words.

86. Mr. Sanchez is having his students work with one-syllable words, removing the first consonant and substituting another, as in m/ats to h/ats. What reading skill are they working on?
(Skill 8.1, Average Rigor)

A. Morphemic inflections.

B. Pronouncing short vowels.

C. Invented spelling.

D. Phonological awareness.

87. Ms. James is seated with a child by her side. The child is reading aloud from an open book. Ms. James is teaching in a school that has embraced the Balanced Literacy Approach. Therefore it is most likely that Ms James is writing and recording:
(Skill 8.1, Average Rigor)

A. The child's use of expression in reading aloud.

B. The child's errors and miscues.

C. Her observations of the child's attitude toward reading.

D. The child's feelings about the particular passage being read.

88. In order to get children to compile specialized vocabulary, they can use:
(Skill 8.2, Average Rigor)

A. Newspapers.

B. Internet resources and approved web-sites that focus on their special interest.

C. Experts they can interview.

D. All of the above.

89. An effective way to build vocabulary and to make connections with mandated science and mathematics material is to teach Greek and Latin roots using:
(Skill 8.2, Average Rigor)

A. Semantic maps.

B. Hierarchical arrays.

C. Linear arrays.

D. Word webs.

90. Cues in reading are:
(Skills 8.3, Average Rigor)

A. Vowel sounds.

B. Digraphs.

C. Sources of information used by readers to help them construct meaning.

D. Tips given by the teacher.

91. In a balanced literacy classroom, new vocabulary would most likely appear on:
(Skill 8.3, Average Rigor)

A. An experiential chart.

B. A class newspaper.

C. The word wall.

D. Outside the room on a bulletin board.

92. As far as the balanced literacy movement is concerned the "WHOLE" is:
(Skill 8.3, Average Rigor)

A. All the reading themes to be covered that day.

B. The whole class meeting for the mini lesson.

C. The complete unit to be covered over the month.

D. All of the reading and writing work to be done in connection with one book.

93. Reviews during the lesson lead to which of the following?
(Skill 8.3, Average Rigor)

A. A loss of class momentum

B. Confusion if done before the students have internalized the subject matter

C. Greater subject matter retention

D. Disjointed lessons

94. How can video laser disks be used in instruction?
(Skill 8.5, Easy)

A. Students can use the laser disk to create pictures for reports

B. Students can use the laser disk to create a science experiment

C. Students can use the laser disk to record class activities

D. Students can use the laser disk to review concepts studied

95. What might be a result if the teacher is distracted by some unrelated event in the instruction?
(Skill 9.1, Easy)

A. Students will leave the class

B. Students will understand the importance of class rules

C. Students will stay on-task longer

D. Students will lose the momentum of the lesson

96. How can student misconduct be redirected at times?
(Skill 9.2, Average Rigor)

A. The teacher threatens the students

B. The teacher assigns detention to the whole class

C. The teacher stops the activity and stares at the students

D. The teacher effectively handles changing from one activity to another

97. Marcus is a first grade boy of good developmental attainment. His learning progress is good the first half of the year. He shows no indicators of emotional distress. After the holiday break, he returns much changed. He is quieter, sullen even, tending to play alone. He has moments of tearfulness, sometimes almost without cause. He avoids contact with adults as often as he can. Even play with his friends has become limited. He has episodes of wetting not seen before, and often wants to sleep in school. What approach is appropriate for this sudden change in behavior? (Skill 9.2, Rigorous)

A. Give him some time to adjust after the holiday break.

B. Report this change immediately to administration. Do not call the parents until administration decides a course of action

C. Document his daily behavior carefully as soon as you notice such a change; report to administration the next month or so in a meeting

D. Make a courtesy call to the parents to let them know he is not acting like himself.

98. The concept of efficient use of time includes which of the following? (Skill 9.2, Average Rigor)

A. Daily review, seatwork, and recitation of concepts

B. Lesson initiation, transition, and comprehension check

C. Review, test, review

D. Punctuality, management transition, and wait time avoidance

99. What is a sample of an academic transition signal? (Skill 9.2, Average Rigor)

A. "How do clouds form?"

B. "Today we are going to study clouds."

C. "We have completed today's lesson."

D. "That completes the description of cumulus clouds. Now we will look at the description of cirrus clouds."

100. What should the teacher do when a student is tapping a pencil on the desk during a lecture? (Skill 9.2, Average Rigor)

A. Stop the lesson and correct the student as an example to other students

B. Walk over to the student and quietly touch the pencil as a signal for the student to stop

C. Announce to the class that everyone should remember to remain quiet during the lecture

D. Ignore the student, hoping he or she will stop

101. What is one way of effectively managing student conduct? (Skill 9.3, Rigorous)

A. State expectations about behavior

B. Let students discipline their peers

C. Let minor infractions of the rules go unnoticed

D. Increase disapproving remarks

102. **The teacher is working with a student. Jane, who is seated at her desk, begins to hit Alan, who sits next to her. The teacher instructs the individual student to keep working, and quietly speaks to Jane. What is the teacher demonstrating?**
(Skill 9.3, Rigorous)

A. Overlap emersion

B. Task-desist overlap

C. Task-intrusion overlap

D. Alternative behavior

103. **While teaching, three students cause separate disruptions. The teacher selects the major one and tells that student to desist. What is the teacher demonstrating?**
(Skill 9.3, Rigorous)

A. Deviancy spread

B. Correct target desist

C. Alternative behavior

D. Desist major deviance

104. **Robert throws a piece of paper across the room. Dennis, sitting next to Robert, bats the piece of paper to the back of the room. The teacher ignores Dennis and reprimands Robert. What is the teacher demonstrating?**
(Skill 9.3, Rigorous)

A. Deviant disruption

B. Correct target desist

C. Alternative behavior

D. Serious desist

105. **To maintain the flow of events in the classroom, what should an effective teacher do?**
(Skill 9.3, Average Rigor)

A. Work only in small groups

B. Use only whole class activities

C. Direct attention to content, rather than focusing the class on misbehavior

D. Follow lectures with written assignments

106. **What is most likely to happen when students witness a punitive or angry desist? (Skill 9.3, Rigorous)**

   A. Respond with more behavior disruption

   B. All disruptive behavior stops

   C. Students align with teacher

   D. Behavior stays the same

107. **What is a teacher statement that implies warmth toward and feeling for the children? (Skill 9.3, Rigorous)**

   A. Roughness of desist

   B. Clarity of desist

   C. Approval-focus desist

   D. Task-focus desist

108. **Which of the following can be measured utilizing the following types of assessments: direct observation, role playing, context observation, and teacher ratings? (Skill 9.3, Easy)**

   A. Social Skills

   B. Reading Skills

   C. Math Skills

   D. Need for specialized instruction

109. **What is an event that increases the likelihood that the response it follows will occur again? (Skill 9.3, Rigorous)**

   A. Stimulus

   B. Unconditioned stimulus

   C. Retrieval cue

   D. Reinforcer

110. **Why is praise for compliance important in classroom management? (Skill 9.3, Average Rigor)**

   A. Students will continue deviant behavior

   B. Desirable conduct will be repeated

   C. It reflects simplicity and warmth

   D. Students will fulfill obligations

111. When planning instruction, which of the following is an organizational tool to help ensure you are providing a well balanced set of objectives?
(Skill 10.1, Rigorous)

A. Using a taxonomy to develop objectives

B. Determining prior knowledge skill levels

C. Determining readiness levels

D. Ensuring you meet the needs of diverse learners

112. When considering the development of the curriculum, which of the following accurately describe the four factors which need to be considered?
(Skill 10.1, Rigorous)

A. Alignment, Scope, Sequence, and Design

B. Assessment, Instruction, Design, and Sequence

C. Data, Alignment, Correlation, and Score

D. Alignment, Sequence, Design and Assessment

113. What do cooperative learning methods all have in common?
(Skill 10.3, Rigorous)

A. Philosophy

B. Cooperative task/cooperative reward structures

C. Student roles and communication

D. Teacher roles

114. What should be considered when evaluating textbooks for content? (Skill 10.3, Easy)

A. Type of print used

B. Number of photos used

C. Free of cultural stereotyping

D. Outlines at the beginning of each chapter

115. Which of the following could be an example of a situation which could have an effect on a student's learning and academic progress?
(Skill 11.1, Average Rigor)

A. Relocation

B. Abuse

C. Both of the Above

D. Neither of the Above

116. Andy shows up to class abusive and irritable. He is often late, sleeps in class, sometimes slurs his speech, and has an odor of drinking. What is the first intervention to take?
(Skill 11.1, Average Rigor)

A. Confront him, relying on a trusting relationship you think you have

B. Do a lesson on alcohol abuse, making an example of him.

C. Do nothing, it is better to err on the side of failing to identify substance abuse

D. Call administration, avoid conflict, and supervise others carefully.

117. A 16 year-old girl who has been looking sad writes an essay in which the main protagonist commits suicide. You overhear her talking about suicide. What do you do?
(Skill 11.1, Average Rigor)

A. Report this immediately to school administration, talk to the girl, letting her know you will talk to her parents about it

B. Report this immediately to authorities

C. Report this immediately to school administration. Make your own report to authorities if required by protocol in your school. Do nothing else

D. Just give the child some extra attention, as it may just be that's all she's looking for

118. You are leading a substance abuse discussion for health class. The students present their belief that marijuana is not harmful to their health. What set of data would refute their claim?
(Skill 11.1, Rigorous)

A. It is more carcinogenic than nicotine, lowers resistance to infection, worsens acne, and damages brain cells

B. It damages brain cells, causes behavior changes in prenatally exposed infants, leads to other drug abuse, and causes short-term memory loss

C. It lowers tolerance for frustration, causes eye damage, increases paranoia, and lowers resistance to infection

D. It leads to abusing alcohol, lowers white blood cell count, reduces fertility, and causes gout

119. Jeanne, a bright, attentive student is in first hour English. She is quiet, but very alert, often visually scanning the room in random patterns. Her pupils are dilated and she has a slight but noticeable tremor in her hands. She fails to note a cue given from her teacher. At odd moments she will act as if responding to stimuli that aren't there by suddenly changing her gaze. When spoken to directly, she has a limited response, but her teacher has a sense she is not herself. What should the teacher do?
(Skill 11.1, Average Rigor)

A. Ask the student if she is all right, then let it go, as there are not enough signals to be alarmed

B. Meet with the student after class to get more information before making a referral

C. Send the student to the office to see the health nurse

D. Quietly call for administration, remain calm and be careful not to alarm the class

120. A parent has left an angry message on the teacher's voicemail. The message relates to a concern about a student and is directed at the teacher. The teacher should: (Skill 11.1, Easy)

   A. Call back immediately and confront the parent

   B. Cool off, plan what to discuss with the parent, then call back

   C. Question the child to find out what set off the parent

   D. Ignore the message, since feelings of anger usually subside after a while

121. Which of the following should NOT be a purpose of a parent-teacher conference? (Skill 11.1, Easy)

   A. To involve the parent in their child's education

   B. To establish a friendship with the child's parents

   C. To resolve a concern about the child's performance

   D. To inform parents of positive behaviors by the child

122. Mr. Brown wishes to improve his parent communication skills. Which of the following is a strategy he can utilize to accomplish this goal? (Skill 11.1, Easy)

   A. Hold parent-teacher conferences

   B. Send home positive notes

   C. Have parent nights where the parents are invited into his classroom

   D. All of the above

124. Bobby, a nine year-old, has been caught stealing frequently in the classroom. What might be a factor contributing to this behavior? (Skill 11.1, Average Rigor)

   A. Need for the items stolen

   B. Serious emotional disturbance

   C. Desire to experiment

   D. A normal stage of development

125. Tommy is a student in your class, his parents are deaf. Tommy is struggling with math and you want to contact the parents to discuss the issues. How should you proceed?
(Skill 11.1, Easy)

A. Limit contact due to the parents inability to hear

B. Use a TTY phone to communicate with the parents

C. Talk to your administrator to find an appropriate interpreter to help you communicate with the parents personally

D. Both B and C but not A

125. Primarily why are operant techniques used in the classroom?
(Skill 11.1, Rigorous)

A. To establish punishments

B. To modify behaviors

C. To change behaviors

D. To establish behaviors

126. According to recent studies, what is the estimated number of adolescents that have physical, social, or emotional problems related to the abuse of alcohol?
(Skill 11.1, Average Rigor)

A. Less that one million

B. 1-2 million

C. 2-3 million

D. Over four million

127. A child exhibits the following symptoms: a lack of emotional responsivity, indifference to physical contact, abnormal social play, and abnormal speech. What is the likely diagnosis for this child?
(Skill 11.1, Average Rigor)

A. Separation anxiety

B. Mental retardation

C. Autism

D. Hypochondria

128. Mrs. Peck wants to justify the use of personalized learning community to her principal. Which of the following reasons should she use?
(Skill 11.2, Rigorous)

A. They build multiculturalism

B. They provide a supportive environment to address academic and emotional needs

C. They builds relationships between students which promote life long learning

D. They are proactive in their nature

129. Johnny, a middle-schooler, comes to class, uncharacteristically tired, distracted, withdrawn, sullen, and cries easily. What would be the teacher's first response?
(Skill 11.2, Easy)

A. Send him to the office to sit

B. Call his parents

C. Ask him what is wrong

D. Ignore his behavior

130. What is an effective way to prepare students for testing?
(Skill 11.6, Average Rigor)

A. Minimize the importance of the test

B. Orient the students to the test, telling them of the purpose, how the results will be used and how it is relevant to them

C. Use the same format for every test are given

D. Have them construct an outline to study from

131. The data coordinator of the district who is concerned with federal funding for reading will probably want to start aggregating scores immediately because:
(Skill 11.7, Rigorous)

A. The public has a right to know.

B. By aggregating, the individual scores can be combined to view performance trends across groups.

C. This will help the district determine which groups need more remedial instruction.

D. B and C.

132. How can students use a computer desktop publishing center?
(Skill 12.1, Easy)

A. To set up a classroom budget

B. To create student made books

C. To design a research project

D. To create a classroom behavior management system

133. When a teacher wants to utilize an assessment which is subjective in nature, which of the following is the most effective method for scoring?
(Skill 13.1, Easy)

A. Rubric

B. Checklist

C. Alternative Assessment

D. Subjective measures should not be utilized

134. Maria was an outstanding student in her elementary school in Brazil. Now she is nervous about starting fourth grade in the US, although she learned English as a second language in Brazil. She and her parents should be relieved to know that:
(Skill 14.1, Rigorous)

A. She will get extra help in the United States with her English.

B. There is a positive and strong correlation between a child's native language and his/her learning of English.

C. Her classmates will help her.

D. She will have a few months to study for the reading test.

135. Safeguards against bias and discrimination in the assessment of children include:
(Skill 14.1, Average Rigor)

A. The testing of a child in standard English

B. The requirement for the use of one standardized test

C. The use of evaluative materials in the child's native language or other mode of communication

D. All testing performed by a certified, licensed, psychologist

136. Which of the following is an accurate description of ESL students? (Skill 14.1, Easy)

A. Remedial students

B. Exceptional education students

C. Are not a homogeneous group

D. Feel confident in communicating in English when with their peers

137. What are the steps of CALLA (Cognitive Academic Language Learning Approach)? (Skill 14.1, Rigorous)

A. Purpose, content, materials, plans

B. Description, sequence, choice, classification, principles, evaluation

C. Sentence structure, content, appearance, organization

D. Preparation, presentation, practice, evaluation, follow-up

138. Etienne is an ESL student. He has begun to engage in conversation which produces a connected narrative. What developmental stage for second language acquisition is he in? (Skill 14.1, Rigorous)

A. Early production

B. Speech emergence

C. Preproduction

D. Intermediate fluency

139. Which of the following describes the functional approach to language acquisition? (Skill 14.2, Average Rigor)

A. Communicative elements

B. Conceptual purposes

C. Grammar elements

D. All of the above

140.   Is it easier for ELL students who read in their first language to learn to read in English? (Skill 14.2, Rigorous)

   A. No, because the letter-sound relationships in English are unique.

   B. Yes, because this will give the children confidence.

   C. No, because there is often interference from one language to the next.

   D. Yes, because the process is the same regardless of the language.

Sample Answer Key

1. B	49. C	97. B
2. B	50. C	98. D
3. B	51. B	99. D
4. D	52. C	100. B
5. D	53. D	101. A
6. D	54. B	102. B
7. D	55. B	103. D
8. B	56. B	104. B
9. B	57. A	105. C
10. C	58. B	106. A
11. A	59. D	107. C
12. B	60. C	108. A
13. A	61. B	109. D
14. B	62. B	110. B
15. C	63. D	111. A
16. A	64. B	112. A
17. B	65. A	113. B
18. B	66. A	114. C
19. C	67. D	115. C
20. B	68. C	116. D
21. C	69. A	117. C
22. C	70. B	118. B
23. C	71. D	119. D
24. C	72. B	120. B
25. C	73. C	121. B
26. B	74. A	122. D
27. C	75. D	123. B
28. B	76. D	124. D
29. B	77. B	125. B
30. D	78. B	126. D
31. C	79. B	127. C
32. A	80. B	128. B
33. D	81. A	129. C
34. C	82. B	130. B
35. D	83. D	131. D
36. B	84. C	132. B
37. C	85. C	133. A
38. B	86. D	134. B
39. C	87. B	135. C
40. C	88. D	136. C
41. D	89. D	137. D
42. A	90. C	138. D
43. D	91. C	139. A
44. A	92. B	140. D
45. B	93. B	
46. A	94. D	
47. D	95. D	
48. B	96. D	

Rigor Table

Easy	Average Rigor	Rigorous
Questions – 4, 11, 12, 16, 22, 37, 41, 44, 46, 60, 73, 77, 78, 79, 82, 85, 94, 95, 108, 114, 120, 121, 122, 124, 129, 132, 133, 136	Questions – 1, 6, 7, 8, 14, 15, 17, 18, 20, 27, 32, 33, 38, 40, 42, 48, 50, 52, 54, 55, 57, 58, 59, 62, 63, 65, 66, 69, 71, 75, 76, 83, 86, 87, 88, 89, 90, 91, 92, 93, 96, 98, 99, 100, 105, 110, 115, 116, 117, 119, 123, 126, 127, 130, 135, 139	Questions – 2, 3, 5, 9, 10, 13, 19, 21, 23, 24, 25, 26, 28, 29, 30, 31, 34, 35, 36, 39, 43, 45, 47, 49, 51, 53, 56, 61, 64, 67, 68, 70, 72, 74, 80, 81, 84, 97, 101, 102, 103, 104, 106, 107, 109, 111, 112, 113, 118, 125, 128, 131, 134, 137, 138, 140

Rationales with Sample Questions

1. **What would improve planning for instruction?**
(Skill 1.1, Average Rigor)

A.   Describe the role of the teacher and student

B.   Evaluate the outcomes of instruction

C.   Rearrange the order of activities

D.   Give outside assignments

Answer: B. Evaluate the outcomes of instruction

Important as it is to plan content, materials, activities, goals taking into account learner needs and to base what goes on in the classroom on the results of that planning, it makes no difference if students are not able to demonstrate improvement in the skills being taught. An important part of the planning process is for the teacher to constantly adapt all aspects of the curriculum to what is actually happening in the classroom. Planning frequently misses the mark or fails to allow for unexpected factors. Evaluating the outcomes of instruction regularly and making adjustments accordingly will have a positive impact on the overall success of a teaching methodology.

2. **What is the best definition for an achievement test?**
(Skill 1.1, Rigorous)

A.   It measures mechanical and practical abilities

B.   It measures broad areas of knowledge that are the result of cumulative learning experiences

C.   It measures the ability to learn to perform a task

D.   It measures performance related to specific, recently acquired information

The correct answer is B: It measures broad areas of knowledge that are the result of cumulative learning experiences.

The ways that a teacher uses test data is a meaningful aspect of instruction and may increase the motivation level of the students especially when this information is available in the form of feedback to the students. This feedback should indicate to the students what they need to do in order to improve their achievement. Frequent testing and feedback is most often an effective way to increase achievement.

3. **Norm-referenced tests:**
   (Skill 1.1, Rigorous)

A. Give information only about the local samples results.

B. Provide information about how the local test takers did compared to a representative sampling of national test takers.

C. Make no comparisons to national test takers.

D. None of the above.

The correct answer is B. Provide information about how the local test takers did compared to a representative sampling of national test takers.

This is the definition of a norm-referenced test.

4. **A standardized test will be:**
   (Skill 1.1, Easy)

A. Given out with the same predetermined questions and format to all.

B. Not be given to certain children.

C. If given out in exactly the same format with the same content, may be taken over a lengthier test period (i.e. 4 hours instead of three or two).

D. All of the above.

The correct answer is D. All of the above.

All of the choices together make up the definition of a standardized test.

5.	Which of the following describes why it is important and necessary for teachers to be able to analyze data on their students? *(Skill 1.2, Rigorous)*

A.	To provide appropriate instruction

B.	To make instructional decisions

C.	To communicate and determine instructional progress

D.	All of the above

Answer: D. All of the above

Especially in today's high stakes environment, it is critical teachers have a complete understanding of the process involved in examining student data in order to make instructional decisions, prepare lessons, determine progress, and report progress to stakeholders.

6.	How are standardized tests useful in assessment? (Skill 1.2, Average Rigor)

A.	For teacher evaluation

B.	For evaluation of the administration

C.	For comparison from school to school

D.	For comparison to the population on which the test was normed

The correct answer is D: For comparison to the population on which the test was normed.

While the efficacy of the standardized tests that are being used nationally has come under attack recently, they are, actually the only device for comparing where an individual student stands with a wide range of peers. They also provide a measure for a program or a school to evaluate how their own students are doing as compared to the populace at large. Even so, they should not be the only measure upon which decisions are made or evaluations drawn. There are many other instruments for measuring student achievement that the teacher needs to consult and take into account.

7. **What is evaluation of the instructional activity based on?**
   (Skill 1.3, Average Rigor)

A. Student grades

B. Teacher evaluation

C. Student participation

D. Specified criteria

The correct answer is D: Specified criteria.

The ways that a teacher uses test data is a meaningful aspect of instruction and may increase the motivation level of the students especially, when this information takes the form of feedback to the students. However, In order for a test to be an accurate measurement of student progress, the teacher must know how to plan and construct tests. Perhaps the most important caveat in creating and using tests for classroom purposes is the old adage to test what you teach. Actually, it is better stated that you should teach what you plan to test. This second phrasing more clearly reflects the need for thorough planning of the entire-instructional program. Before you begin instruction, you should have the assessment planned and defined. One common method of matching the test to the instruction is to develop a table of specifications, a two-way grid in which the objectives of instruction are listed on one axis and the content that has been presented is listed on the other axis. Then the individual cells are assigned percentages that reflect the focus and extent of instruction in each area. The final step is to distribute the number of questions to be used on the test among the cells of the table in proportion to the identified percentages.

8. **What must be a consideration when a parent complains that he/she can't control their child's behavior?**
(Skill 1.3, Average Rigor)

A. Consider whether the parent gives feedback to the child

B. Consider whether the parent's expectations for control are developmentally appropriate

C. Consider how much time the parent spends with the child

D. Consider how rigid the rules are that the parent sets

The correct answer is B: Consider whether the parent's expectations for control are developmentally appropriate.

The teacher is the expert when it comes to developmental expectations. This is one area where a concerned and helpful teacher can be invaluable in helping a family through a crisis. Parents often have unrealistic expectations about their children's behavior simply because they don't know what is normal and what is not. Some stages tend to be annoying, especially if they are not understood. A teacher can help to defuse the conflicts in these cases.

9. **If teachers attend to content, instructional materials, activities, learner needs, and goals in instructional planning, what could be an outcome?**
(Skill 1.3, Rigorous)

A. Planning for the next year

B. Effective classroom performance

C. Elevated test scores on standardized tests

D. More student involvement

The correct answer is B: Effective classroom performance.

Another outcome will be teacher satisfaction in a job well-done and in the performance of her students. Her days will have far fewer disruptions and her classroom will be easy to manage.

10. **Mrs. Grant is providing her students with many extrinsic motivators in order to increase their intrinsic motivation. Which of the best explains this relationship?**
(Skill 1.4, Rigorous)

A.   This is a good relationship and will increase intrinsic motivation

B.   The relationship builds animosity between the teacher and the students

C.   Extrinsic motivation does not in itself help to build intrinsic motivation

D.   There is no place for extrinsic motivation in the classroom

Answer: C. Extrinsic motivation does not in itself help to build intrinsic motivation

There are some cases where it is necessary to utilize extrinsic motivation; however, the use of extrinsic motivation is not alone a strategy to use to build intrinsic motivation. Intrinsic motivation comes from within the student themselves, while extrinsic motivation comes from outside parties.

11. **Which of the following is considered a study skill?**
(Skill 1.4, Easy)

A.   Using graphs, tables, and maps

B.   Using a desk-top publishing program

C.   Explaining important vocabulary words

D.   Asking for clarification

The correct answer is A: Using graphs, tables, and maps.

In studying, it is certainly true that "a picture is worth a thousand words." Not only are these devices useful in making a point clear, they are excellent mnemonic devices for remembering facts.

12. **Which of the following test items is not objective?**
(Skill 1.4, Easy)

A.   Multiple choice

B.   Essay

C.   Matching

D.   True/false

The correct answer is B: Essay.

Measuring outcomes may be the most challenging task a new teacher faces. Planning is important here as in all other aspects of classroom management. The test items used in typical classroom tests are either objective questions or essay questions. The drawback to this test item is the possible ambiguity of student-supplied answers. Another common form of objective question is the true/false test item. Gronlund and Linn point out that some limitations to this test item is its susceptibility to guessing, the difficulty involved in constructing a true/false item that is valid, and the limited specific learning outcomes it can measure. However, they also point out its usefulness in identifying cause and effect relationships as well as distinguishing fact and opinion. A third form of test item is the matching exercise. An advantage of this type of test item is its ability to test large blocks of material in a short time. The major problem with this type of test item is its emphasis on memorization. Kenneth H. Hoover does not favor this type of test item but points out that it can be appropriate when the exercise contains at least five, but not more than twelve items, uses only homogeneous items, and contains at least three extra answers to choose from.

The most commonly used objective question where the student chooses an answer is the multiple-choice question. The multiple-choice test item consists of a stem and a list of responses, of which only one is the best answer. The choices that are not the correct answer are called distracters. Gronlund and Linn point out that multiple-choice test items are most useful for specific learning outcomes that utilize the student's ability to understand or interpret factual information. Since the multiple-choice test item can be adopted to most subject matter, and because of its versatile nature, it is the most commonly used item on standardized tests. However, as Gronlund and Linn point out, the multiple-choice test item cannot test the ability to organize and present ideas.

13. **What should a teacher do when students have not responded well to an instructional activity?**
(Skill 2.1, Rigorous)

A. Reevaluate learner needs

B. Request administrative help

C. Continue with the activity another day

D. Assign homework on the concept

The correct answer is A: Reevaluate learner needs.

The value of teacher observations cannot be underestimated. It is through the use of observations that the teacher is able to informally assess the needs of the students during instruction. These observations will drive the lesson and determine the direction that the lesson will take based on student activity and behavior. After a lesson is carefully planned, teacher observation is the single most important component of an instructional presentation. If the teacher observes that a particular student is not on-task, she will change the method of instruction accordingly. She may change from a teacher-directed approach to a more interactive approach. Questioning will increase in order to increase the participation of the students. If appropriate, the teacher will introduce manipulative materials to the lesson. In addition, teachers may switch to a cooperative group activity, thereby removing the responsibility of instruction from the teacher and putting it on the students.

14.   **Why is it important for a teacher to pose a question before calling on students to answer?**
      (Skill 2.1, Average Rigor)

A.   It helps manage student conduct

B.   It keeps the students as a group focused on the class work

C.   It allows students time to collaborate

D.   It gives the teacher time to walk among the students

The correct answer is B: It keeps the students as a group focused on the class work.

It doesn't take much distraction for a class's attention to become diffused. Once this happens, effectively teaching a principle or a skill is very difficult. The teacher should plan presentations that will keep students focused on the lesson. A very useful tool is effective, well-thought-out, pointed questions.

15.   **Which statement is an example of specific praise?**
      (Skill 2.1, Average Rigor)

A.   "John, you are the only person in class not paying attention"

B.   "William, I thought we agreed that you would turn in all of your homework"

C.   "Robert, you did a good job staying in line. See how it helped us get to music class on time"

D.   "Class, you did a great job cleaning up the art room"

The correct answer is C: "Robert, you did a good job staying in line. See how it helped us get to music class on time?"

Praise is a powerful tool in obtaining and maintaining order in a classroom. In addition, it is an effective motivator. It is even more effective if the positive results of good behavior are included.

16.   **What is one way a teacher can supplement verbal praise? (Skill 2.1, Easy)**

A.   Help students evaluate their own performance and supply self-reinforcement

B.   Give verbal praise more frequently

C.   Give tangible rewards such as stickers or treats

D.   Have students practice giving verbal praise

The correct answer is A: Help students evaluate their own performance and supply self-reinforcement.

While praise is useful in maintaining order in a classroom and in motivating students, it's important for the teacher to remember at all times that one major educational objective is that of preparing students to succeed in the world once the supports of the classroom are gone. Self-esteem or lack of it are often barriers to success. An important lesson and skill for students to learn is how to bolster one's own self-esteem and confidence.

17.   **The teacher states that students will review the material from the previous day, demonstrate an electronic circuit, and set up an electronic circuit in small groups. What has the teacher demonstrated? (Skill 2.1, Average Rigor)**

A.   The importance of reviewing

B.   Giving the general framework for the lesson to facilitate learning

C.   Giving students the opportunity to leave if they are not interested in the lesson

D.   Providing momentum for the lesson

The correct answer is B: Giving the general framework for the lesson to facilitate learning.

If children know where they're going, they're more likely to be engaged in getting there. It's important to give them a road map whenever possible for what is coming in their classes.

18. **What is one benefit of amplifying a student's response? (Skill 2.1, Average Rigor)**

A.   It helps the student develop a positive self-image

B.   It is helpful to other students who are in the process of learning the reasoning or steps in answering the question

C.   It allows the teacher to cover more content

D.   It helps to keep the information organized

The correct answer is B: It is helpful to other students who are in the process of learning the reasoning or steps in answering the question.

Not only does the teacher show acceptance and give value to student responses by acknowledging, amplifying, discussing or restating the comment or question, she also helps the rest of the class learn to reason. If a student response is allowed, even if it is blurted out, it must be acknowledged and the student made aware of the quality of the response. A teacher acknowledges a student response by commenting on it. For example, the teacher states the definition of a noun, and then asks for examples of nouns in the classroom. A student responds, "My pencil is a noun." The teacher answers, "Okay, let us list that on the board." By this response and the action of writing "pencil" on the board, the teacher has just incorporated the student's response into the lesson. A teacher may also amplify the student response through another question directed to either the original student or to another student. For example, the teacher may say, "Okay," giving the student feedback on the quality of the answer, and then add, "What do you mean by "run" when you say the battery runs the radio?" Another way of showing acceptance and value of student response is to discuss the student response. For example, after a student responds, the teacher would say, "Class, let us think along that line. What is some evidence that proves what Susie just stated?" The teacher may also restate the response. For example, the teacher might say, "So you are saying the seasons are caused by the tilt of the earth. Is this what you said?"

19. **When is optimal benefit reached when handling an incorrect student response?**
(Skill 2.1, Rigorous)

A.   When specific praise is used

B.   When the other students are allowed to correct that student

C.   When the student is redirected to a better problem solving approach

D.   When the teacher asks simple questions, provides cues to clarify, or gives assistance for working out the correct response

The correct answer is C: When the student is redirected to a better problem solving approach.

It's important that students feel confident and comfortable in making responses, knowing that even if they give a wrong answer, they will not be embarrassed. If a student is ridiculed or embarrassed by an incorrect response, the student my shut down and not participate thereafter in classroom discussion. One way to respond to the incorrect answer is to ask the child, "Show me from your book why you think that." This gives the student a chance to correct the answer and redeem himself or herself. Another possible response from the teacher is to use the answer as a non-example. For example, after discussing the characteristics of warm-blooded and cold-blooded animals, the teacher asks for some examples of warm-blooded animals. A student raises his or her hand and responds, "A snake." The teacher could then say, "Remember, snakes lay eggs; they do not have live births. However, a snake is a good non-example of a mammal." The teacher then draws a line down the board and under a heading of "non-example" writes "snake." This action conveys to the child that even though the answer was wrong, it still contributed positively to the class discussion. Notice how the teacher did not digress from the task of listing warm-blooded animals, which in other words is maintaining academic focus, and at the same time allowed the student to maintain dignity.

20. How can the teacher help students become more work oriented and less disruptive?
(Skill 2.1, Average Rigor)

A.   Seek their input for content instruction

B.   Challenge the students with a task and show genuine enthusiasm for it

C.   Use behavior modification techniques with all students

D.   Make sure lesson plans are complete for the week

The correct answer is B: Challenge the students with a task and show genuine enthusiasm for it.

Many studies have demonstrated that the enthusiasm of the teacher is infectious. If students feel that the teacher is ambivalent about a task, they will also catch that attitude.

21. What has been established to increase student originality, intrinsic motivation, and higher order thinking skills?
(Skill 2.1, Rigorous)

A.   Classroom climate

B.   High expectations

C.   Student choice

D.   Use of authentic learning opportunities

Answer: C. Student choice

While all of the descriptors are good attributes for students to demonstrate, it has been shown through research that providing student choice can increase all of the described factors.

22. **What is an example of formative feedback?**
(Skill 2.1, Easy)

A.   The results of an intelligence test

B.   Correcting the tests in small groups

C.   Verbal behavior that expresses approval of a student response to a test item

D.   Scheduling a discussion prior to the test

The correct answer is C: Verbal behavior that expresses approval of a student response to a test item.

Standardized testing is currently under great scrutiny but educators agree that any test that serves as a means of gathering and interpreting information about children's learning and which can provide accurate, helpful input for nurturing children's further growth, is acceptable. All testing must be formative in nature. Formative evaluation is the basic, everyday kind of assessment that teachers continually do to understand students' growth and to help them learn further.

23. **Why is it important for the teacher to alert non-performers when conducting activities?**
(Skill 2.1, Rigorous)

A.   It creates suspense

B.   Students will take over the discipline

C.   Students will become more work involved

D.   Students will more likely not take part in the recitation

The correct answer is C: Students will become more work involved.

Students are eager to shift into neutral gear when they are not specifically involved in an activity, which is a waste of classroom time for those students. The teacher needs to find ways to keep them involved in what is going on even if they are only spectators.

24.   Mrs. Shapiro states, "During the past four weeks we have discussed national and international conditions which led to the outbreak of World War II. Tomorrow we are going to spend some time going over them again and comparing and contrasting them with conditions in the world today. Make a list of these conditions from your class notes, and let's see how complete our lists are." What is this an example of?
(Skill 2.1, Rigorous)

A.   Topic summary within the lesson

B.   Weekly summary and recap

C.   Lesson-end review

D.   Test preparation

The correct answer is C: Lesson-end review.

Lesson-end reviews are restatements (by the teacher or teacher and students) of the content of discussion at the end of a lesson. The research shows that effective teachers use reviews and recaps on a daily basis in the classroom. T. Good and D.A. Grouws determined the effectiveness of forty teachers by looking at the achievement records of their students from various classes. They established a list of key variables that separates the effective teachers from the ineffective teachers. The list includes a daily review covering the concepts and skills contained in the homework, giving further practice while the teacher deals with the homework, followed by a comprehension check of the homework concepts before proceeding with the day. Also on the list of key concepts are special reviews conducted weekly and monthly. The weekly reviews are conducted every Monday morning and focus on the skills and concepts of the previous week. The monthly reviews are conducted once a month and focus on skills and concepts from the previous month's lessons. Moreover, they reported the teachers utilizing the reviews to complement daily learning were significantly more successful in inducing student subject matter retention than the ineffective teachers.

The idea of regularly scheduled reviews is encouraged. Beginning teachers are advised to maintain a structured classroom. This is because too many of today's students come from disjointed families. It is possible that the only structure in a student's life may be in the classroom. Therefore, doing a daily review of the homework for the first few minutes of class followed by a few minutes of practice sets up a routine that the student can feel comfortable with. Moreover, when students know what is coming next and what is expected of them, they feel more a part of their learning environment and deviant behavior is lessened.

25. **Ms. Smith says, "Yes, exactly what do you mean by "It was the author's intention to mislead you." What does this illustrate? (Skill 2.1, Rigorous)**

A. Digression

B. Restates response

C. Probes a response

D. Amplifies a response

The correct answer is C: Probes a response.

From ancient times notable teachers such as Socrates and Jesus have employed oral-questioning to enhance their discourse, to stimulate thinking, and/or to stir emotion among their audiences. Educational researchers and practitioners virtually all agree that teachers' effective use of questioning promotes student learning. Effective teachers continually develop their questioning skills.

26. **What is a frequently used type of feedback to students? (Skill 2.1, Rigorous)**

A. Correctives

B. Simple praise-confirmation

C. Correcting the response

D. Explanations

The correct answer is B: Simple praise—confirmation.

Even if the student's answer is not perfect, there are always ways to praise him and to make use of his answer unless, of course, he was deliberately answering wrongly. When a behavior is praised, it is likely to be repeated.

**27.   What can be concluded from research on concept teaching?
(Skill 2.1, Average Rigor)**

A.   The most effective way is oral presentation and visual examples

B.   The most effective way is to use manipulatives and oral presentation

C.   The most effective way is to use a definition with examples and non-examples

D.   The most effective way is to use visuals and manipulatives

The correct answer is C: The most effective way is to use a definition with examples and non-examples.

In presenting explanatory knowledge, the teacher relates an outcome as is expected from a principle or law. This is a much more complicated teaching strategy and learning process than acquiring concepts. Students will not necessarily attain knowledge when the teacher states an academic law. It is essential for the teacher to explain the law in common terms that the students can easily understand. Often this explanation will be followed by a group discussion. Teachers can facilitate students' comprehension of laws or principles by analyzing causal conditions and their effects.

**28.   What is the definition of a non-performer?
(Skill 2.1, Rigorous)**

A.   Students who are off-task

B.   Students not chosen to answer a teacher-posed question

C.   Students with stanine scores of 20 or below

D.   Students who consistently score below 50 percent on classroom tests

The correct answer is B: Students not chosen to answera teacher-posed question.

Not all students can answer every question, of course. However, the teacher should be careful that all students do participate and that no student is permitted to be passive in all discussion periods.

29.	**What is not a way that teachers show acceptance and give value to a student response?**
	(Skill 2.1, Rigorous)

A.	Acknowledging

B.	Correcting

C.	Discussing

D.	Amplifying

The correct answer is B. Correcting.

There are ways to treat every answer as worthwhile even if it happens to be wrong. The objective is to keep students involved in the dialogue. If their efforts to participate are "rewarded" with what seems to them to be a rebuke or that leads to embarrassment, they will be less willing to respond the next time.

30. **What is teacher with-it-ness?**
     (Skill 2.1, Rigorous)

A.   Having adequate knowledge of subject matter

B.   A skill that must be mastered to attain certification

C.   Understanding the current fads and trends that affect students

D.   Attending to two tasks at once

The correct answer is D: Attending to two tasks at once.

The teacher who knows his/her class well and is "with-it" will be cognizant of what is happening in every corner of the classroom between and among the children at all times. It should be relatively easy to identify problems that occur during the school day since the teacher observes the students as they interact with one another. Should the teacher be unaware of problems between students, misbehavior will surely occur. At this point in time the teacher will then tune in to the child who is misbehaving and hopefully, will soon be able to see what is happening to cause misbehaviors. As with anything else, the best way to solve behavior problems is to prevent them. The "with-it" teacher frequently knows when and why problems will occur and will act to eliminate potential provocation. The simplest means of preventing conflict between students who are having a problem with one another is to give them their own space and to separate them. Teacher with-it-ness is defined as "teacher behavior that indicates to the students that the teacher knows what they are doing" at all times and at the same time can continue instruction. With-it-ness has been found to positively affect both classroom behavior management and student task involvement. Teachers who have been specially trained in with-it-ness, report positive correlation between their with-it-ness and reading achievement as well as reductions in student misbehaviors and disruptions. Teacher training in with-it-ness techniques includes:

a)   implementing positive questioning techniques
b)   using alerting cues
c)   giving goal-directed prompts
d)   using a soft voice when making reprimands
e)   integrating alternative behavior desists
f)   applying concurrent and specific praise

Research in regard to teacher with-it-ness indicate that teachers who are comfortable with the above techniques and are "with-it" increase instructional time by at least twenty minutes per day and decrease deviant behavior significantly. Further, with-it-ness techniques have been found to apply to boys as well as girls, to emotionally disturbed children as well as non-disturbed children, and to both younger and older grade children. They also apply to the entire class as well as to individual students.

31. **The teacher responds, "Yes, that is correct" to a student's answer. What is this an example of?**
    (Skill 2.1, Rigorous)

A. Academic feedback

B. Academic praise

C. Simple positive response

D. Simple negative response

The correct answer is C: Simple positive response.

The reason for praise in the classroom is to increase the desirable in order to eliminate the undesirable. This refers to both conduct and academic focus. It further states that effective praise should be authentic, it should be used in a variety of ways, and it should be low-keyed. Academic praise is a group of specific statements that give information about the value of the response or its implications. For example, a teacher using academic praise would respond, "That is an excellent analysis of Twain's use of the river in Huckleberry Finn." Whereas a simple positive response to the same question would be: "That's correct."

32. **Which of the following is not a characteristic of effective praise? (Skill 2.1, Average Rigor)**

A.   Praise is delivered in front of the class so it will serve to motivate others

B.   Praise is low-key

C.   Praise provides information about student competence

D.   Praise is delivered contingently

The correct answer is A: Praise is delivered in front of the class so it will serve to motivate others.

The reason for praise in the classroom is to increase the desirable in order to eliminate the undesirable. This refers to both conduct and academic focus. It further states that effective praise should be authentic, it should be used in a variety of ways, and it should be low-keyed. Academic praise is a group of specific statements that give information about the value of the response or its implications. For example, a teacher using academic praise would respond, "That is an excellent analysis of Twain's use of the river in Huckleberry Finn." Whereas a simple positive response to the same question would be: "That's correct."

33. **What are teacher redirects?**
    (Skill 2.1, Average Rigor)

A.   The teacher redirects the deviant behavior to another task

B.   The teacher changes the focus of the class to provide smooth transitions

C.   The teacher changes student jobs every nine weeks

D.   The teacher asks a second student to expound on the first student's answer

The correct answer is D: The teacher asks a second student to expound on the first student's answer.

Beginning-teacher training explains that the focus of the classroom discussion should be on the subject matter and controlled by teacher-posed questions. When a student response is correct, it is not difficult to maintain academic focus. However, when the student response is incorrect, this task is a little more difficult. The teacher must redirect the discussion to the task at hand, and at the same time not devalue the student response. It is risky to respond in a classroom. If a student is ridiculed or embarrassed by an incorrect response, the student my shut down and not participate thereafter in classroom discussion. One way to respond to the incorrect answer is to ask the child, "Show me from your book why you think that." This gives the student a chance to correct the answer and redeem himself or herself. Another possible response from the teacher is to use the answer as a non-example. For example, after discussing the characteristics of warm-blooded and cold-blooded animals, the teacher asks for some examples of warm-blooded animals. A student raises his or her hand and responds, "A snake." The teacher could then say, "Remember, snakes lay eggs; they do not have live birth. However, a snake is a good non-example of a mammal." The teacher then draws a line down the board and under a heading of "non-example" writes "snake." This action conveys to the child that even though the answer was wrong, it still contributed positively to the class discussion. Notice how the teacher did not digress from the task of listing warm-blooded animals, which in other words is maintaining academic focus, and at the same time allowed the student to maintain dignity.

**34.   Discovery learning is to inquiry as direct instruction is to…
(Skill 2.3, Rigorous)**

A.   Scripted lessons

B.   Well-developed instructions

C.   Clear instructions which eliminate all misinterpretations

D.   Creativity of teaching

Answer: C. Clear instructions which eliminate all misinterpretations

Direct instruction is a technique which relies on carefully well developed instructions and lessons which eliminate misinterpretations. In this manner, all students have the opportunity to acquire and learn the skills presented to the students. This approach limits teacher creativity to some extent, but has a good solid research based following with much ability to replicate its results.

**35.   The concept of efficient use of time includes which of the following?
(Skill 2.3, Rigorous)**

A.   Daily review, seatwork, and recitation of concepts

B.   Lesson initiation, transition, and comprehension check

C.   Review, test, review

D.   Punctuality, management transition, and wait time avoidance

Answer: D. Punctuality, management transition, and wait time avoidance

The "benevolent boss" described in the rationale for question 34 applies here. One who succeeds in managing a business follows these rules; so does the successful teacher.

36. **The success oriented classroom is designed to ensure students are successful at attaining new skills. In addition, mistakes are viewed as… in this type of classroom.**
    (Skill 2.3, Rigorous)

A.   Motivations to improve

B.   Natural part of the learning process

C.   Ways to improve

D.   Building blocks

Answer: B. Natural part of the learning process.

In the success oriented classroom, mistakes are viewed as a natural part of learning. In this way, mistakes continue the learning. Students have the ability to continually improve their grades or learning by correcting mistakes, rather than the mistake being a penalty.

37. **Which of the following can impact the desire of students to learn new material?**
    (Skill 2.3, Easy)

A.   Assessments plan

B.   Lesson plans

C.   Enthusiasm

D.   School community

Answer: C. Enthusiasm

The enthusiasm a teacher exhibits can not only have positive effects on students' desire to learn, but also on on-task behaviors as well.

38.   How can mnemonic devices be used to increase achievement? (Skill 2.3, Average Rigor)

A.   They help the child rehearse the information

B.   They help the child visually imagine the information

C.   They help the child to code information

D.   They help the child reinforce concepts

The correct answer is B: They help the child visually imagine the information.

Mnemonics are often verbal, something such as a very short poem or a special word used to help a person remember something, particularly lists. Mnemonics rely not only on repetition to remember facts, but also on associations between easy-to-remember constructs and lists of data, based on the principle that the humanistic mind much more easily remembers insignificant data attached to spatial, personal, or otherwise meaningful information than that occurring in meaningless sequences (like Kool-Aid). The sequences must make sense, though. If a random mnemonic is made up, it is not necessarily a memory aid.

39.   What is the definition of proactive classroom management? (Skill 2.3, Rigorous)

A.   Management that is constantly changing

B.   Management that is downplayed

C.   Management that gives clear and explicit instructions and rewarding compliance

D.   Management that is designed by the students

The correct answer is C: Management that gives clear and explicit instructions and rewards compliance.

Classroom management plans should be in place when the school year begins. Developing a management plan takes a proactive approach—that is, decide what behaviors will be expected of the class as a whole, anticipate possible problems, and teach the behaviors early in the school year. Involving the students in the development of the classroom rules lets the students know the rationale for the rules, allows them to assume responsibility in the rules because they had a part in developing them.

40. **What is the most significant development emerging in children at age two?**
(Skill 2.4, Average Rigor)

A.   Immune system develops

B.   Socialization occurs

C.   Language develops

D.   Perception develops

The correct answer is C: Language develops.

Language begins to develop in an infant not long after birth. Chomsky claims that children teach themselves to speak using the people around them for resources. Several studies of the sounds infants make in their cribs seems to support this. The first stage of meaningful sounds is the uttering of a word that obviously has meaning for the child, for example, "bird" when the child sees one flying through the air. Does the development of real language begin when the noun is linked with a verb ("bird fly")? When language begins and how it develops has been debated for a long time. It's useful for a teacher to investigate those theories and studies.

41. **When communicating with parents for whom English is not the primary language you should:**
(Skill 2.4, Easy)

A.   Provide materials whenever possible in their native language

B.   Use an interpreter

C.   Provide the same communication as you would to native English speaking parents

D.   All of the above

Answer: D. All of the above

When communicating with non English speaking parents it is important to treat them as you would any other parent and utilize any means necessary to ensure they have the ability to participate in their child's educational process.

42. **What has research shown to be the effect of using advance organizers in the lesson?**
     (Skill 2.4, Average Rigor)

A.   They facilitate learning and retention

B.   They enhance retention only

C.   They only serve to help the teacher organize the lesson

D.   They show definitive positive results on student achievement

The correct answer is A: They facilitate learning and retention.

J.M. Kallison, Jr. found subject matter retention increased when lessons included an outline at the beginning of the lesson and a summary at the end of the lesson. This type of structure is utilized in successful classrooms.

43. **When developing lessons it is imperative teachers provide equity in pedagogy so…**
     (Skill 3.1, Rigorous)

A.   Unfair labeling of students will occur

B.   Student experiences will be positive

C.   Students will achieve academic success

D.   All of the above

Answer: D. All of the above

Providing equity of pedagogy allows for students to have positive learning experiences, achieve academic success, and helps to prevent the labeling of students in an unfair manner.

44. **What is a benefit of frequent self-assessment?**
(Skill 3.1, Easy)

A. Opens new venues for professional development

B. Saves teachers the pressure of being observed by others

C. Reduces time spent on areas not needing attention

D. Offers a model for students to adopt in self-improvement

Answer: A. Opens new venues for professional development

When a teacher is involved in the process of self-reflection and self-assessment, one of the common outcomes is that the teacher comes to identify areas of skill or knowledge that require more research or improvement on her part. She may become interested in overcoming a particular weakness in her performance or may decide to attend a workshop or consult with a mentor to learn more about a particular area of concern.

45. **Mrs. Graham has taken the time to reflect, complete observations, and asked for feedback about the interactions between her and her students from her principal. It is obvious by seeking this information out that Mrs. Graham understands which of the following?**
(Skill 3.2, Rigorous)

A. The importance of clear communication with the principal

B. She needs to analyze her effectiveness of classroom interactions

C. She is clearly communicating with the principal

D. She cares about her students

Answer: B. She needs to analyze her effectiveness of classroom interactions

Utilizing reflection, observations and feedback from peers or supervisors, teachers can help to build their own understanding of how they interact with students. In this way, they can better analyze their effectiveness at building appropriate relationships with students.

46. **Which of the following is a good reason to collaborate with a peer: (Skill 3.2, Easy)**

A. To increase your knowledge in areas where you feel you are weak, but the peer is strong

B. To increase your planning time and that of your peer by combining the classes and taking more breaks

C. To have fewer lesson plans to write

D. To teach fewer subjects

Answer: A. To increase your knowledge in areas where you feel you are weak, but the peer is strong

Collaboration with a peer allows teachers to share ideas and information. In this way, the teacher is able to improve his/her skills and share additional information with each other.

47. **Which of the following are ways a professional can assess his/her teaching strengths and weaknesses? (Skill 3.2, Rigorous)**

A. Examining how many students were unable to understand a concept

B. Asking peers for suggestions or ideas

C. Self-evaluation/Reflection of lessons taught

D. All of the above

Answer: D. All of the above

It is important for teachers to involve themselves in constant periods of reflection and self-reflection to ensure they are meeting the needs of the students.

48.   What would improve planning for instruction?
(Skill 4.1, Average Rigor)

A.   Describe the role of the teacher and student

B.   Evaluate the outcomes of instruction

C.   Rearrange the order of activities

D.   Give outside assignments

The correct answer is B: Evaluate the outcomes of instruction.

Important as it is to plan content, materials, activities, goals taking into account learner needs and to base what goes on in the classroom on the results of that planning, it makes no difference if students are not able to demonstrate improvement in the skills being taught. An important part of the planning process is for the teacher to constantly adapt all aspects of the curriculum to what is actually happening in the classroom. Planning frequently misses the mark or fails to allow for unexpected factors. Evaluating the outcomes of instruction regularly and making adjustments accordingly will have a positive impact on the overall success of a teaching methodology.

49.   Which of the following type of question will not stimulate higher-level
critical thinking?
(Skill 4.1 Rigorous)

A.   A hypothetical question

B.   An open-ended question

C.   A close-ended question

D.   A judgment question

The correct answer is C. A close-ended question.

The answer is C. A close-ended question requires a simple answer, like a "yes" or "no." An open-ended question can generate an extended response that would require critical thinking. Both a hypothetical question and a judgment question require deeper thinking skills.

50. Which of the following is <u>not</u> one of the levels of Bloom's taxonomy?
(Skill 4.1, Average Rigor)

A.   Synthesis

B.   Evaluation

C.   Understanding

D.   Knowledge

Answer: C. Understanding

Bloom's taxonomy consists of the following levels: knowledge, comprehension, application, analysis, synthesis, evaluation. These levels are in order from the most basic level to the more complex.

51. Mr. Ryan has proposed to his classroom that the students may demonstrate understanding of the unit taught in a variety of ways including: taking a test, writing a paper, creating an oral presentation, or building a model/project. Which of the following areas of differentiation has Mr. Ryan demonstrated?
(Skill 4.1, Rigorous)

A.   Synthesis

B.   Product

C.   Content

D.   Product

Answer: B. Product

There are three ways to differentiate instruction: content, process, product. In the described case, Mr. Ryan has chosen to provide the students with alternate opportunities to produce knowledge; therefore, the product is the area being differentiated.

52. **What is an example of a low order question?**
     (Skill 4.1, Average Rigor)

A.   "Why is it important to recycle items in your home?"

B.   "Compare how glass and plastics are recycled."

C.   "What items do we recycle in our county?"

D.   "Explain the importance of recycling in our county.

The correct answer is C: "What items do we recycle in our county?"

Remember that the difference between specificity and abstractness is a continuum. The most specific is something that is concrete and can be seen, heard, smelled, tasted, or felt, like cans, bottles, and newspapers. At the other end of the spectrum is an abstraction like importance. Lower-order questions are on the concrete end of the continuum; higher-order questions are on the abstract end.

53. **Which of the following is an example of a synthesis question**
     according to Bloom's taxonomy?
     (Skill 4.1, Rigorous)

A.   "What is the definition
        of_____?"

B.   "Compare _____ to _____."

C.   "Match column A to column
        B."

D.   "Propose an alternative
        to_____."

The correct answer is D: "Propose an alternative to_____."

There are six levels to the taxonomy: Knowledge, Comprehension, Application, Analysis, Synthesis, and Evaluation. Synthesis is compiling information together in a different way by combining elements in a new pattern or proposing alternative solutions to produce a unique communication, plan, or proposed set of operations or to derive a set of abstract relations.

54. **When is content teaching effective?**
(Skill 4.1, Average Rigor)

A. When it is presented in demonstration form

B. When the teacher separates the content into distinct elements

C. When the content is covered over a long span of time

D. When the decision about content is made at the district level

The correct answer is B: When the teacher separates the content into distinct elements.

Students of all ages can absorb material that is focused better than material that is diffuse. Structuring the presentation of new material by topics and staying on target within each component is the most effective way to communicate material that students will be expected to use in some way—in performing tasks or in taking tests.

55. Wait-time has what effect?
(Skill 4.2, Average Rigor)

A. Gives structure to the class discourse

B. Fewer chain and low level questions are asked with more higher level questions included

C. Gives the students time to evaluate the response

D. Gives the opportunity for in-depth discussion about the topic

The correct answer is B. Fewer chain and low level questions are asked with more higher level questions included.

One part of the questioning process for the successful teacher is *wait-time*: the time between the question and either the student response or your follow-up. Many teachers vaguely recommend some general amount of wait-time (until the student starts to get uncomfortable or is clearly perplexed), but we focus here on wait-time as a specific and powerful communicative tool that speaks through its structured silences. Embedded in wait-time are subtle clues about your judgments of a student's abilities and your expectations of individuals and groups. For example, the more time you allow a student to mull through a question, the more you trust his or her ability to answer that question without getting flustered. As a rule, the practice of prompting is not a problem. Giving support and helping students reason through difficult conundrums is part of being an effective teacher.

56. **What is an effective amount of "wait time"?**
(Skill 4.2, Rigorous)

A.   1 second

B.   5 seconds

C.   15 seconds

D.   10 seconds

The correct answer is B: 5 seconds.

In formal training, most pre-service teachers are taught the art of questioning. One part of the questioning process is *wait-time*: the time between the question and either the student response or your follow-up. Many teachers vaguely recommend some general amount of wait-time (until the student starts to get uncomfortable or is clearly perplexed), but we focus here on wait-time as a specific and powerful communicative tool that speaks through its structured silences. Embedded in wait-time are subtle clues about your judgments of a student's abilities and your expectations of individuals and groups. For example, the more time you allow a student to mull through a question, the more you trust his or her ability to answer that question without getting flustered.
As a rule, the practice of prompting is not a problem. Giving support and helping students reason through difficult conundrums is part of being an effective teacher.

57. **How can the teacher establish a positive climate in the classroom?**
(Skill 5.1, Average Rigor)

A.   Help students see the unique contributions of individual differences

B.   Use whole group instruction for all content areas

C.   Help students divide into cooperative groups based on ability

D.   Eliminate teaching strategies that allow students to make choices

The correct answer is A: Help students see the unique contributions of individual differences.

In the first place, an important purpose of education is to prepare students to live successfully in the real world, and this is an important insight and understanding for them to take into that world. In the second place, the most fertile learning environment is one in which all viewpoints and backgrounds are respected and where everyone has equal respect.

58. **What do cooperative learning methods all have in common?**
(Skill 5.1, Average Rigor)

A. Philosophy

B. Cooperative task/cooperative reward structures

C. Student roles and communication

D. Teacher roles

The correct answer is B: Cooperative task/cooperative reward structures.

Cooperative learning situations, as practiced in today's classrooms, grew out of searches conducted by several groups in the early 1970's. Cooperative learning situations can range from very formal applications such as STAD (Student Teams-Achievement Divisions) and CIRC (Cooperative Integrated Reading and Composition) to less formal groupings known variously as "group investigation," "learning together," and "discovery groups." Cooperative learning as a general term is now firmly recognized and established as a teaching and learning technique in American schools. Since cooperative learning techniques are so widely diffused in the schools, it is necessary to orient students in the skills by which cooperative learning groups can operate smoothly, and thereby enhance learning. Students who cannot interact constructively with other students will not be able to take advantage of the learning opportunities provided by the cooperative learning situations and will furthermore deprive their fellow students of the opportunity for cooperative learning.

59. **What is a good strategy for teaching ethnically diverse students?**
(Skill 5.2, Average Rigor)

A. Don't focus on the students' culture

B. Expect them to assimilate easily into your classroom

C. Imitate their speech patterns

D. Include ethnic studies in the curriculum

The correct answer is D: Include ethnic studies in the curriculum.

Exploring students' own cultures increases their confidence levels in the group. It is also a very useful tool when students are struggling to develop identities that they can feel comfortable with. The bonus is that this is good training for living in the world.

60. **Which of the following is an example of a restriction within the affective domain?**
(Skill 5.2, Easy)

A. Unable to think abstractly

B. Inability to synthesize information

C. Inability to concentrate

D. Inability complete physical activities

Answer: C. Inability to concentrate

The affective domain refers to such things as concentration, focus, lack of participation, inability to express themselves, and inconsistent behavior. Areas of the affective domain may affect other domains such as the cognitive or physical.

61. **What developmental patterns should a professional teacher assess to meet the needs of the student?**
(Skill 6.1, Rigorous)

A. Academic, regional, and family background

B. Social, physical, academic

C. Academic, physical, and family background

D. Physical, family, ethnic background

The correct answer is B: Social, physical, academic.

The effective teacher applies knowledge of physical, social, and academic developmental patterns and of individual differences, to meet the instructional needs of all students in the classroom and. The most important premise of child development is that all domains of development (physical, social, and academic) are integrated. The teacher has a broad knowledge and thorough understanding of the development that typically occurs during the students' current period of life. More importantly, the teacher understands how children learn best during each period of development. An examination of the student's file coupled with ongoing evaluation assures a successful educational experience for both teacher and students.

62. **Which is true of child protective services?**
    (Skill 6.2, Average Rigor)

A.   They have been forced to become more punitive in their attempts to treat and prevent child abuse and neglect

B.   They have become more a means for identifying cases of abuse and less an agent for rehabilitation due to the large volume of cases

C.   They have become advocates for structured discipline within the school

D.   They have become a strong advocate in the court system

The correct answer is B: They have become more a means for identifying cases of abuse and less an agent for rehabilitation due to the large volume of cases.

Nina Bernstein, who wrote *The Lost Children of Wilder* told of a long-running lawsuit in New York City that attempted to hold the city and its child-care services responsible for meeting the needs of abused children. Unfortunately, while it is an extreme case, it is not untypical of the plight of children all across the country. The only thing a teacher can do is attempt to provide a refuge of concern and stability during the time such children are in her care, hoping that they will, somehow, survive.

63. **Students who can solve problems mentally have...**
    (Skill 7.1, Average Rigor)

A.   Reached maturity

B.   Physically developed

C.   Reached the pre-operational stage of thought

D.   Achieved the ability to manipulate objects symbolically

Answer: D. Achieved the ability to manipulate objects symbolically

When students are able to solve mental problems, it is an indication to the teacher that they have achieved the ability to manipulate objects symbolically and should be instructed to continue to develop their cognitive and academic skills.

64. **Mrs. Potts has noticed an undercurrent in her classroom of an unsettled nature. She is in the middle of her math lesson, but still notices that many of her students seem to be having some sort of difficulty. Mrs. Potts stops class and decides to have a class meeting. She understands that even though her math objectives are important, it is equally important to address whatever is troubling her classroom. What is it Mrs. Potts knows?**
   (Skill 7.1, Rigorous)

   A.   Discipline is important

   B.   Social issues can impact academic learning

   C.   Maintaining order is important

   D.   Social skills instruction is important.

Answer: B. Social issues can impact academic learning

Mrs. Potts understands that as long as there is a social situation or issue in the classroom, it is unlikely that any academics she presents will be learned. All of those areas instructed are important; however, it is this understanding of the fact that the academics will be impacted that is important in this particular situation as she is interrupting her math instruction.

65. **In successful inclusion of students with disabilities:**
(Skill 7.1, Average Rigor)

A.   A variety of instructional arrangements are available

B.   School personnel shift the responsibility for learning outcomes to the student

C.   The physical facilities are used as they are

D.   Regular classroom teachers have sole responsibility for evaluating student progress

Answer: A. A variety of instructional arrangements are available

Here are some support systems and activities that are in evidence where successful inclusion has occurred:

Attitudes and beliefs
- the regular teacher believes the student can succeed.
- school personnel are committed to accepting responsibility for the learning outcomes of students with disabilities.
- school personnel and the students in the class have been prepared to receive a student with disabilities

Services and Physical accommodations
- services needed by the student are available (e.g. health, physical, occupational, or speech therapy).
- accommodations to the physical plant and equipment are adequate to meet the students' needs (e.g. toys, building and playground facilities, learning materials, assistive devices).

School support
- the principal understands the needs of students with disabilities
- adequate numbers of personnel, including aides and support personnel, are available
- adequate staff development and technical assistance, based on the needs of the school personnel, are being provided (e.g. information on disabilities, instructional methods, awareness and acceptance activities for students and team-building skills).
- appropriate policies and procedures for monitoring individual student progress, including grading and testing are in place

Collaboration
- special educators are part of the instructional or planning team
- teaming approaches are used for program implementation and problem solving
- regular teachers, special education teachers, and other specialists collaborate (e.g. co-teach, team teach, work together on teacher assistance teams).

Instructional methods
- teachers have the knowledge and skills needed to select and adapt curricular and instructional methods according to individual student needs
- a variety of instructional arrangements is available (e.g. team teaching, cross-grade grouping, peer tutoring, teacher assistance teams).
- teachers foster a cooperative learning environment and promote socialization.

66. **Which of the following is not a communication issue that is related to diversity within the classroom?**
(Skill 7.2, Average Rigor)

A. Learning disorder

B. Sensitive terminology

C. Body language

D. Discussing differing viewpoints and opinions

Answer: A. Learning disorders

Learning disorders, while they may have a foundation in the specific communication skills of a student, are not in and of themselves a communication issue related to diversity within the classroom.

67. **When are students more likely to understand complex ideas? (Skill 7.3, Rigorous)**

A. If they do outside research before coming to class

B. Later when they write out the definitions of complex words

C. When they attend a lecture on the subject

D. When they are clearly defined by the teacher and are given examples and nonexamples of the concept

The correct answer is D: When they are clearly defined by the teacher and are given examples and nonexamples of the concept.

Several studies have been carried out to determine the effectiveness of giving examples as well as the difference in effectiveness of various types of examples. It was found conclusively that the most effective method of concept presentation included giving a definition along with examples and non-examples and also providing an explanation of them. These same studies indicate that boring examples were just as effective as interesting examples in promoting learning. Additional studies have been conducted to determine the most effective number of examples that will result in maximum student learning. These studies concluded that a few thoughtfully selected examples are just as effective as many examples. It was determined that the actual number of examples necessary to promote student learning was relative to the learning characteristics of the learners. It was again ascertained that learning is facilitated when examples are provided along with the definition.

68.   What have recent studies regarding effective teachers concluded? (Skill 7.3, Rigorous)

A.   Effective teachers let students establish rules

B.   Effective teachers establish routines by the sixth week of school

C.   Effective teachers state their own policies and establish consistent class rules and procedures on the first day of class

D.   Effective teachers establish flexible routines

The correct answer is C: Effective teachers state their own policies and establish consistent class rules and procedures on the first day of class.

The teacher can get ahead of the game by stating clearly on the first day of school in her introductory information for the students exactly what the rules. These should be stated firmly but unemotionally. When one of those rules is broken, he/she can then refer to the rules, rendering enforcement much easier to achieve. It's extremely difficult to achieve goals with students who are out of control. Establishing limits early and consistently enforcing them enhances learning. It is also helpful for the teacher to display prominently the classroom rules. This will serve as a visual reminder of the students' expected behaviors. In a study of classroom management procedures, it was established that the combination of conspicuously displayed rules, frequent verbal references to the rules, and appropriate consequences for appropriate behaviors led to increased levels of on-task behavior.

69. **When is utilization of instructional materials most effective?**
(Skill 7.3, Average Rigor)

A. When the activities are sequenced

B. When the materials are prepared ahead of time

C. When the students choose the pages to work on

D. When the students create the instructional materials

Answer: A. When the activities are sequenced

Most assignments will require more than one educational principle. It is helpful to explain to students the proper order in which these principles must be applied to complete the assignment successfully. Subsequently, students should also be informed of the nature of the assignment (i.e., cooperative learning, group project, individual assignment, etc). This is often done at the start of the assignment.

70. **If teachers attend to content, instructional materials, activities, learner needs, and goals in instructional planning, what could be an outcome?**
(Skill 7.3, Rigorous)

A. Planning for the next year

B. Effective classroom performance

C. Elevated test scores on standardized tests

D. More student involvement

Answer: B. Effective classroom performance

Another outcome will be teacher satisfaction in a job well-done and in the performance of her students. Her days will have far fewer disruptions and her classroom will be easy to manage.

71. **When creating and selecting materials for instruction, teachers should complete which of the following steps:**
(Skill 7.3, Average Rigor)

A. Relevant to the prior knowledge of the students

B. Allow for a variation of learning styles

C. Choose alternative teaching strategies

D. All of the above

Answer: D. All of the above

It is imperative that when creating and selecting materials for instruction that teachers consider many different factors. This makes the planning for instruction a difficult and somewhat time consuming process. There are numerous factors which must always be balanced in order to deliver the most appropriate and beneficial instruction to students.

72. **The teacher states, "We will work on the first page of vocabulary words. On the second page we will work on the structure and meaning of the words. We will go over these together and then you will write out the answers to the exercises on your own. I will be circulating to give help if needed". What is this an example of?**
(Skill 7.3, Rigorous)

A. Evaluation of instructional activity

B. Analysis of instructional activity

C. Identification of expected outcomes

D. Pacing of instructional activity

The correct answer is B: Analysis of instructional activity.

The successful teacher carefully plans all activities to foresee any difficulties in executing the plan. This also assures that the directions being given to students will be clear, avoiding any misunderstanding.

73. **According to Piaget, what stage is characterized by the ability to think abstractly and to use logic?**
(Skill 7.4, Easy)

A. Concrete operations

B. Pre-operational

C. Formal operations

D. Conservative operational

The correct answer is C: Formal operations.

The four development stages are described in Piaget's theory as follows:
1. Sensorimotor stage: from birth to age 2 years (children experience the world through movement and senses).
2. Preoperational stage: from ages 2 to 7 (acquisition of motor skills).
3. Concrete operational stage: from ages 7 to 11 (children begin to think logically about concrete events).
4. Formal operational stage: after age 11 (development of abstract reasoning).

These chronological periods are approximate and, in light of the fact that studies have demonstrated great variation between children, cannot be seen as rigid norms. Furthermore, these stages occur at different ages, depending upon the domain of knowledge under consideration. The ages normally given for the stages reflect when each stage tends to predominate even though one might elicit examples of two, three, or even all four stages of thinking at the same time from one individual, depending upon the domain of knowledge and the means used to elicit it.

74. **At approximately what age is the average child able to define abstract terms such as honesty and justice?**
(Skill 7.4, Rigorous)

A.   10-12 years old

B.   4-6 years old

C.   14-16 years old

D.   6-8 years old

The answer is A: 10-12 years old.

The usual age for the fourth stage (the formal operational stage) as described by Piaget is from 10 to 12 years old. It is in this stage that children begin to be able to define abstract terms.

75. **According to Piaget's theory of cognitive development, what is the process of incorporating new objects, information or experiences into the existing cognitive structures?**
(Skill 7.4, Average Rigor)

A.   Attachment

B.   Conservation

C.   Identification

E.   Assimilation

The answer is D: Assimilation.

Piaget felt that development from one stage to the next is caused by the accumulation of errors in the child's understanding of the environment; this accumulation eventually causes such a degree of cognitive disequilibrium that thought structures require reorganizing. Once knowledge is constructed internally, it is then tested against reality the same way a scientist tests the validity of hypotheses. Like a scientist, the individual learner may discard, modify, or reconstruct knowledge based on its utility in the real world. Much of this construction (and later reconstruction) is, in fact, done subconsciously; however, once reconstruction has occurred, the conclusion is assimilated and becomes a feature of the child's personality.

76. **Which of following is not the role of the teacher in the instructional process:**
   (Skill 7.4, Average Rigor)

A.   Instructor

B.   Coach

C.   Facilitator

D.   Follower

Answer: D. Follower

The teacher demonstrates a variety of roles within the classroom. Teachers, however, should not be followers. They must balance all of their roles in an efficient way to ensure that instruction is delivered to meet the needs of his/her students.

77. **How many stages of intellectual development does Piaget define?**
   (Skill 7.4, Easy)

A.   Two

B.   Four

C.   Six

D.   Eight

The correct answer is B: Four.

The stages are:
1.   <u>Sensorimotor stage</u>: from birth to age 2 years (children experience the world through movement and senses).
2.   <u>Preoperational stage</u>: from ages 2 to 7(acquisition of motor skills).
3.   <u>Concrete operational stage</u>: from ages 7 to 11 (children begin to think logically about concrete events).
4.   <u>Formal Operational stage</u>: after age 11 (development of abstract reasoning).

78.   **When using a kinesthetic approach, what would be an appropriate activity?**
        (Skill 7.4, Easy)

A.   List

B.   Match

C.   Define

D.   Debate

The correct answer is B: Match.

Brain lateralization theory emerged in the 1970s and demonstrated that the left hemisphere appeared to be associated with verbal and sequential abilities whereas the right hemisphere appeared to be associated with emotions and with spatial, holistic processing. Although those particular conclusions continue to be challenged, it is clear that people concentrate, process, and remember new and difficult information under very different conditions. For example, auditory and visual perceptual strengths, passivity, and self-oriented or authority-oriented motivation often correlate with high academic achievement, whereas tactual and kinesthetic strengths, a need for mobility, nonconformity, and peer motivation often correlate with school underachievement (Dunn & Dunn, 1992, 1993). Understanding how students perceive the task of learning new information differently is often helpful in tailoring the classroom experience for optimal success.

79. **Who developed the theory of multiple intelligences?**
(Skill 7.4, Easy)

A.   Bruner

B.   Gardner

C.   Kagan

D.   Cooper

The correct answer is B: Gardner.

Howard Gardner's most famous work is probably *Frames of Mind*, which details seven dimensions of intelligence (Visual/Spatial Intelligence, Musical Intelligence, Verbal Intelligence, Logical/Mathematical Intelligence, Interpersonal Intelligence, Intrapersonal Intelligence, and Bodily/Kinesthetic Intelligence). Gardner's claim that pencil and paper IQ tests do not capture the full range of human intelligences has garnered much praise within the field of education but has also met criticism, largely from psychometricians. Since the publication of *Frames of Mind*, Gardner has additionally identified the 8th dimension of intelligence: Naturalist Intelligence, and is still considering a possible ninth—Existentialist Intelligence.

80. Piaget's learning theory asserts that adolescents in the formal operations period…
(Skill 7.4 , Rigorous)

A.   Behave properly from fear of punishment rather than from a conscious decision to take a certain action.

B.   See the past more realistically and can relate to people from the past more than preadolescents.

C.   Are less self-conscious and thus more willing to project their own identities into those of fictional characters.

D.   Have not yet developed a symbolic imagination.

The correct answer is B. See the past more realistically and can relate to people from the past more than preadolescents.

The answer is B, since according to Piaget, adolescents 12-15 years old begin thinking beyond the immediate and obvious, and theorize. Their assessment of events shifts from considering an action as "right" or "wrong" to considering the intent and behavior in which the action was performed. Fairy tale or other kinds of unreal characters have ceased to satisfy them and they are able to recognize the difference between pure history and historical fiction.

81. **According to Piaget, what is a child born with?**
(Skill 7.4, Rigorous)

A. The tendency to actively relate pieces of information acquired

B. The ability to adapt

C. Primary emotions

D. Desire

The correct answer is A: The tendency to actively relate pieces of information acquired.

The four development stages are described in Piaget's theory as follows:
5. Sensorimotor stage: from birth to age 2 years (children experience the world through movement and senses).
6. Preoperational stage: from ages 2 to 7 (acquisition of motor skills).
7. Concrete operational stage: from ages 7 to 11 (children begin to think logically about concrete events).
8. Formal operational stage: after age 11 (development of abstract reasoning).
9.
These chronological periods are approximate and, in light of the fact that studies have demonstrated great variation between children, cannot be seen as rigid norms. Furthermore, these stages occur at different ages, depending upon the domain of knowledge under consideration. The ages normally given for the stages reflect when each stage tends to predominate even though one might elicit examples of two, three, or even all four stages of thinking at the same time from one individual, depending upon the domain of knowledge and the means used to elicit it.

82. **Which of the following is a presentation modification?**
(Skill 7.5, Easy)

A. Taking an assessment in an alternate room

B. Providing an interpreter to give the test in American Sign Language

C. Allowing dictation of written responses

D. Extending the time limits on an assessment

Answer: B. Providing an interpreter to give the test in American Sign Language

There are numerous types of modifications which can be provided to students in the classroom and for assessments. All of the described choices are appropriate modifications, but the only one which effects the presentation of the items is the one related to providing an interpreter.

83.   **According to Piaget, when does the development of symbolic functioning and language take place?**
        (Skill 7.4, Average Rigor)

A.   Concrete operations stage

B.   Formal operations stage

C.   Sensorimotor stage

D.   Preoperational stage

The correct answer is D: Preoperational stage.

Although there is no general theory of cognitive development, the most historically influential theory was developed by Jean Piaget, a Swiss psychologist (1896-1980). His theory provided many central concepts in the field of developmental psychology. His theory concerned the growth of intelligence, which for Piaget meant the ability to more accurately represent the world and perform logical operations on representations of concepts grounded in the world. His theory concerns the emergence and acquisition of schemata—schemes of how one perceives the world—in "developmental stages," times when children are acquiring new ways of mentally representing information. His theory is considered "constructivist," meaning that, unlike nativist theories (which describe cognitive development as the unfolding of innate knowledge and abilities) or empiricist theories (which describe cognitive development as the gradual acquisition of knowledge through experience), asserts that we construct our cognitive abilities through self-motivated action in the world. For his development of the theory, Piaget was awarded the Erasmus Prize.

84. **What would the presence of a low attention span and restlessness in a child be a possible indication of?**
(Skill 7.5, Rigorous)

A.   Anger

B.   Retardation

C.   Hyperkinesis

D.   Adaptation

The correct answer is C: Hyperkinesis.

Attention-deficit hyperactivity disorder (ADHD) as a cause of hyperkinesis (hyperactivity) has received a lot of attention in recent years. However, other conditions can cause it as well. Normal young children can be very lively and have short attention spans. Normal teenagers can also appear hyperactive; puberty can cause it. Children who are bored, are suffering from mental conflict, or are having problems at home, which may even include sexual abuse, can be hyperactive. The disorder has a large range of affects on children. Some have learning disabilities, while others may be very gifted. Hyperactivity can also occur because of problems with hearing or vision. Overactive thyroid, lead poisoning, depression, anxiety, and a range of psychiatric illnesses are some of the potential causes. Hyperactivity is sometimes associated with mania. Another more common cause of hyperactivity is lack of sleep. More severe cases of hyperactivity can be very harmful if left untreated, since hyperactive people seldom think about the consequences of their actions.

85.   **The major difference between phonemic and phonological awareness is:**
      (Skill 8.1, Easy)

A.   One deals with a series of discrete sounds and the other with sound-spelling relationships.

B.   One is involved with teaching and learning alliteration and rhymes.

C.   Phonemic awareness is a specific type of phonological awareness that deals with separate phonemes within a given word.

D.   Phonological awareness is associated with printed words.

The correct answer is C. Phonemic awareness is a specific type of phonological awareness that deals with separate phonemes within a given word.

By definition, phonemic awareness falls under the phonological awareness umbrella. All of the other choices do not deal with the DIFFERENCE between the two types of awareness.

86.   **Mr. Sanchez is having his students work with one-syllable words, removing the first consonant and substituting another, as in m/ats to h/ats. What reading skill are they working on?**
      (Skill 8.1, Average Rigor)

A.   Morphemic inflections.

B.   Pronouncing short vowels.

C.   Invented spelling.

D.   Phonological awareness.

The correct answer is D. Phonological Awareness.
While there are inflections ("s") and short vowels)"a") in these words as in Answers "A" and "B," neither is the focus of this activity. These words have standard spellings, not invented as in Answer "C."

87. **Ms. James is seated with a child by her side. The child is reading aloud from an open book. Ms. James is teaching in a school that has embraced the Balanced Literacy Approach. Therefore it is most likely that Ms James is writing and recording:**
    (Skill 8.1, Average Rigor)

A. The child's use of expression in reading aloud.

B. The child's errors and miscues.

C. Her observations of the child's attitude toward reading.

D. The child's feelings about the particular passage being read.

The correct answer is B. The child's errors and miscues.

This question requires knowledge of running records and familiarity with error recording and miscues. The test taker has to know that this is the standard format for a running record of reading behaviors and that choices "C" and "D" deal with attitudes and feelings which are not part of the running records used as part of the balanced literacy approach.

88. **In order to get children to compile specialized vocabulary, they can use:**
    (Skill 8.2, Average Rigor)

A. Newspapers.

B. Internet resources and approved web-sites that focus on their special interest.

C. Experts they can interview.

D. All of the above.

The correct answer is D. All of the above.

The answer is "D" because all of the responses are correct.

89. An effective way to build vocabulary and to make connections with mandated science and mathematics material is to teach Greek and Latin roots using:
(Skill 8.2, Average Rigor)

A. Semantic maps.

B. Hierarchical arrays.

C. Linear arrays.

D. Word webs.

The correct answer is D. Word webs.

Historically, these have been used to teach Greek and Latin roots

90. Cues in reading are:
(Skills 8.3, Average Rigor)

A. Vowel sounds.

B. Digraphs.

C. Sources of information used by readers to help them construct meaning.

D. Tips given by the teacher.

The correct answer is C. Sources of information used by readers to help them construct meaning.

Cues are sources of information used by readers to help them to understand what they are reading.

91. **In a balanced literacy classroom, new vocabulary would most likely appear on:**
(Skill 8.3, Average Rigor)

A. An experiential chart.

B. A class newspaper.

C. The word wall.

D. Outside the room on a bulletin board.

The correct answer is C. The word wall.

The answer can only be "C" and should be part of the test taker's theoretical background.

92. **As far as the balanced literacy movement is concerned the "WHOLE" is:**
(Skill 8.3, Average Rigor)

A. All the reading themes to be covered that day.

B. The whole class meeting for the mini lesson.

C. The complete unit to be covered over the month.

D. All of the reading and writing work to be done in connection with one book.

The correct answer is B. The whole class meeting for the mini lesson.

This is another deliberately tricky question, since all of the answers make sense, but only "B" is correct because that is the definition of "WHOLE" in balanced literacy.

93.   **Reviews during the lesson lead to which of the following?**
       (Skill 8.3, Average Rigor)

A.   A loss of class momentum

B.   Confusion if done before the students have internalized the subject matter

C.   Greater subject matter retention

D.   Disjointed lessons

The correct answer is B: Confusion if done before the students have internalized the subject matter.

Much research has been conducted on the effects of review on student comprehension and retention, and the most productive approach has consistently been a pre-review and a post-review of the material being covered. If the teacher will do this repeatedly and as a matter of course, students will come to expect it, which will lead not only to orderly classrooms but will help students to take an orderly approach to their own study habits.

94.   **How can video laser disks be used in instruction?**
       (Skill 8.5, Easy)

A.   Students can use the laser disk to create pictures for reports

B.   Students can use the laser disk to create a science experiment

C.   Students can use the laser disk to record class activities

D.   Students can use the laser disk to review concepts studied

The correct answer is D: Students can use the laser disk to review concepts studied.

The teacher's arms are never long enough to render all the help that is needed when students are learning new concepts and practicing skills. Audiovisual aids such as the laser disk extend her arms. Students who need more times through an idea or a skill to master it can have that without the teacher's having to work one on one with a single student or with a classroom of students.

95. **What might be a result if the teacher is distracted by some unrelated event in the instruction?**
(Skill 9.1, Easy)

A.   Students will leave the class

B.   Students will understand the importance of class rules

C.   Students will stay on-task longer

D.   Students will lose the momentum of the lesson

The correct answer is D: Students will lose the momentum of the lesson.

The teacher who can attend to a task situation and an extraneous situation simultaneously without becoming immersed in either one is said to have "with-it-ness." This ability is absolutely imperative for teacher effectiveness and success. It can be a difficult task to address deviant behavior while sustaining academic flow, but this is a skill that teachers need to develop early in their careers and one that will become second nature, intuitive, instinctive. Teacher with-it-ness is defined as "teacher behavior that indicates to the students that the teacher knows what she is doing" at all times and at the same time can continue instruction. With-it-ness has been found to positively affect both classroom behavior management and student task involvement. Teachers who have been specially trained in with-it-ness, report positive correlation between their with-it-ness and reading achievement as well as reductions in student misbehaviors and disruptions.

96. **How can student misconduct be redirected at times?**
(Skill 9.2, Average Rigor)

A.   The teacher threatens the students

B.   The teacher assigns detention to the whole class

C.   The teacher stops the activity and stares at the students

D.   The teacher effectively handles changing from one activity to another

The answer is D: The teacher effectively handles changing from one activity to another.

Appropriate verbal techniques include a soft non-threatening voice void of undue roughness, anger, or impatience regardless of whether the teacher is instructing, providing student alerts, or giving a behavior reprimand. Verbal techniques that may be effective in modifying student behavior, include simply stating the student's name, explaining briefly and succinctly what the student is doing that is inappropriate and what the student should be doing. Verbal techniques for reinforcing behavior include both encouragement and praise delivered by the teacher. In addition, for verbal techniques to positively affect student behavior and learning, the teacher must give clear, concise directives while implying her warmth toward the students.

97. Marcus is a first grade boy of good developmental attainment. His learning progress is good the first half of the year. He shows no indicators of emotional distress. After the holiday break, he returns much changed. He is quieter, sullen even, tending to play alone. He has moments of tearfulness, sometimes almost without cause. He avoids contact with adults as often as he can. Even play with his friends has become limited. He has episodes of wetting not seen before, and often wants to sleep in school. What approach is appropriate for this sudden change in behavior? (Skill 9.2, Rigorous)

A. Give him some time to adjust after the holiday break.

B. Report this change immediately to administration. Do not call the parents until administration decides a course of action

C. Document his daily behavior carefully as soon as you notice such a change; report to administration the next month or so in a meeting

D. Make a courtesy call to the parents to let them know he is not acting like himself.

The correct answer is B: Report this change immediately to administration. Do not call the parents until administration decides a course of action.

Anytime a child's disposition, attitude, or habits change significantly, teachers and parents need to seriously consider the existence of emotional difficulties. Emotional disturbances in childhood are not uncommon and take a variety of forms. Usually these problems show up in the form of uncharacteristic behaviors. Most of the time, children respond favorably to brief treatment programs of psychotherapy. At other times, disturbances may need more intensive therapy and are harder to resolve. All stressful behaviors need to be addressed, and any type of chronic antisocial behavior needs to be examined as a possible symptom of deep-seated emotional upset. In a case where the change is sudden and dramatic, administration needs to become involved.

98. **The concept of efficient use of time includes which of the following? (Skill 9.2, Average Rigor)**

A. Daily review, seatwork, and recitation of concepts

B. Lesson initiation, transition, and comprehension check

C. Review, test, review

D. Punctuality, management transition, and wait time avoidance

The correct answer is D: Punctuality, management transition, and wait time avoidance.

The "benevolent boss" described in the rationale for question 34 applies here. One who succeeds in managing a business follows these rules; so does the successful teacher.

99. **What is a sample of an academic transition signal? (Skill 9.2, Average Rigor)**

A. "How do clouds form?"

B. "Today we are going to study clouds."

C. "We have completed today's lesson."

D. "That completes the description of cumulus clouds. Now we will look at the description of cirrus clouds."

The correct answer is D: "That completes the description of cumulus clouds. Now we will look at the description of cirrus clouds."

Transitions are language bridges between one topic and another. The teacher should thoughtfully plan transitions when several topics are going to be presented in one lesson to be sure that students are carried along. Without transitions, sometimes students are still focused on a previous topic and are lost in the discussion.

100. **What should the teacher do when a student is tapping a pencil on the desk during a lecture?**
(Skill 9.2, Average Rigor)

A.   Stop the lesson and correct the student as an example to other students

B.   Walk over to the student and quietly touch the pencil as a signal for the student to stop

C.   Announce to the class that everyone should remember to remain quiet during the lecture

D.   Ignore the student, hoping he or she will stop

The correct answer is B: Walk over to the student and quietly touch the pencil as a signal for the student to stop.

An assertive discipline plan should be developed as soon as the teacher meets the students. The students can become involved in developing and discussing the needs for the rules. Rules should be limited to four to six basic classroom rules that are simple to remember and positively stated (For example, raise hand to speak, instead of, don't talk without permission).

1.   Recognize and remove roadblocks to assertive discipline. Replace negative expectations with positives, and set reasonable limits for the children.

2.   Practice an assertive response style. That is, clearly state teacher expectations and expect the students to comply with them.

3.   Set limits. Take into consideration the students' behavioral needs, the teacher's expectations, and set limits for behavior. Decide what you will do when the rules are broken or complied with.

4.   Follow through promptly with the consequences when students break the rules. However, the students should clearly know in advance what to expect when a rule is broken. Conversely, also follow through with the promised rewards for compliance and good behavior. This reinforces the concept that individuals choose their behavior and that there are consequences for their behavior.

5.   Devise a system of positive consequences. Positive consequences do not have to always be food or treats. However, rewards should not be promised if it is not possible to deliver them. The result is a more positive classroom.

101. **What is one way of effectively managing student conduct?**
(Skill 9.3, Rigorous)

A.   State expectations about behavior

B.   Let students discipline their peers

C.   Let minor infractions of the rules go unnoticed

D.   Increase disapproving remarks

The correct answer is A: State expectations about behavior.

The effective teacher demonstrates awareness of what the entire class is doing and is in control of the behavior of all students even when the teacher is working with only a small group of the children. In an attempt to prevent student misbehaviors the teacher makes clear, concise statements about what is happening in the classroom directing attention to content and the students' accountability for their work rather than focusing the class on the misbehavior. It is also effective for the teacher to make a positive statement about the appropriate behavior that is observed. If deviant behavior does occur, the effective teacher will specify who the deviant is, what he or she is doing wrong, and why this is unacceptable conduct or what the proper conduct would be. This can be a difficult task to accomplish as the teacher must maintain academic focus and flow while addressing and desisting misbehavior. The teacher must make clear, brief statements about the expectations without raising his/her voice and without disrupting instruction.

102. **The teacher is working with a student. Jane, who is seated at her desk, begins to hit Alan, who sits next to her. The teacher instructs the individual student to keep working, and quietly speaks to Jane. What is the teacher demonstrating?**
(Skill 9.3, Rigorous)

A.   Overlap emersion

B.   Task-desist overlap

C.   Task-intrusion overlap

D.   Alternative behavior

The correct answer is B: Task-desist overlap.

Research indicates that soft reprimands are more effective in controlling disruptive behavior than loud reprimands and that when soft reprimands are used, fewer are needed. The findings of studies of desist techniques (Kounin and Alden, 1970) include: elementary students who witness a punitive or angry desist respond with more behavior disruptions; high school students who witnessed a desist with roughness not only felt discomfort but also regarded the disruption as more serious and at the same time lost focus on the lesson; when a simple reprimand was observed, students felt the teacher was fairest and able to maintain control of the class while preserving academic focus.

103. **While teaching, three students cause separate disruptions. The teacher selects the major one and tells that student to desist. What is the teacher demonstrating?**
(Skill 9.3, Rigorous)

A. Deviancy spread

B. Correct target desist

C. Alternative behavior

D. Desist major deviance

The correct answer is D: Desist major deviance.

When the teacher attempts to desist a deviancy, what he/she says and how it is said directly influence the probability of stopping the misbehavior. The effective teacher demonstrates awareness of what the entire class is doing and is in control of the behavior of all students even when the teacher is working with only a small group of children. In an attempt to prevent student misbehaviors the teacher makes clear, concise statements about what is happening in the classroom directing attention to content and the students' accountability for their work rather than focusing the class on the misbehavior. It is also effective for the teacher to make a positive statement about the appropriate behavior that is observed. If deviant behavior does occur, the effective teacher will specify who the deviant is, what he or she is doing wrong, and why this is unacceptable conduct or what the proper conduct would be. When more than one student is disrupting the class, it is wise to focus on the one that is causing the greatest problem. This is usually sufficient to bring the others into line. This can be a difficult task to accomplish as the teacher must maintain academic focus and flow while addressing and desisting misbehavior. The teacher must make clear, brief statements about the expectations without raising his/her voice and without disrupting instruction.

104. **Robert throws a piece of paper across the room. Dennis, sitting next to Robert, bats the piece of paper to the back of the room. The teacher ignores Dennis and reprimands Robert. What is the teacher demonstrating?**
(Skill 9.3, Rigorous)

A. Deviant disruption

B. Correct target desist

C. Alternative behavior

D. Serious desist

The correct answer is B: Correct target desist.

Students expect fairness from their teacher. By focusing on the student who initiated the misbehavior, the teacher demonstrates fairness in dealing with rule-breakers.

105. **To maintain the flow of events in the classroom, what should an effective teacher do?**
(Skill 9.3, Average Rigor)

A. Work only in small groups

B. Use only whole class activities

C. Direct attention to content, rather than focusing the class on misbehavior

D. Follow lectures with written assignments

The correct answer is C: Direct attention to content, rather than focusing the class on misbehavior.

Students who misbehave often do so to attract attention. By focusing the attention of the misbehaver as well as the rest of the class on the real purpose of the classroom sends the message that misbehaving will not be rewarded with class attention to the misbehaver. Engaging students in content by using the various tools available to the creative teacher goes a long way in ensuring a peaceful classroom.

106. **What is most likely to happen when students witness a punitive or angry desist?**
(Skill 9.3, Rigorous)

A.   Respond with more behavior disruption

B.   All disruptive behavior stops

C.   Students align with teacher

D.   Behavior stays the same

The correct answer is A: Respond with more behavior disruption.

When the teacher becomes angry, several things happen. Students feel that the one who made her angry has achieved his/her goal by misbehaving. They also feel that the teacher is not in control. Because the teacher has become emotional, students feel that they may also react emotionally. Students tend to sympathize with the target of the teacher's anger. The proverb, *A soft word turns away wrath,* certainly applies in the classroom.

107. **What is a teacher statement that implies warmth toward and feeling for the children?**
(Skill 9.3, Rigorous)

A.   Roughness of desist

B.   Clarity of desist

C.   Approval-focus desist

D.   Task-focus desist

The correct answer is C: Approval-focus desist

Everyone wants approval, and that is a powerful message where students are concerned. If they like their teacher and believe that their teacher likes them and approves of them, many of the classical battles of the classroom are avoided. A little bit of praise goes a long way in achieving cooperation.

108. **Which of the following can be measured utilizing the following types of assessments: direct observation, role playing, context observation, and teacher ratings?**
(Skill 9.3, Easy)

A.   Social Skills

B.   Reading Skills

C.   Math Skills

D.   Need for specialized instruction

Answer: A. Social Skills

Social skills can be measured using the listed types of assessments. They can also be measured using sociometric measures including: peer nomination, peer rating, paired-comparison.

109. **What is an event that increases the likelihood that the response it follows will occur again?**
(Skill 9.3, Rigorous)

A.   Stimulus

B.   Unconditioned stimulus

C.   Retrieval cue

D.   Reinforcer

The correct answer is D: Reinforcer.

If a child misbehaves and his peers laugh, the behavior has been reinforced and is likely to happen again. The teacher needs to stop misbehaviors before they start when at all possible. However, the same principle applies with appropriate behavior. The teacher can influence repetitions of the behaviors she wants by reinforcing them when they occur. She can also create circumstances where she has an opportunity to reinforce good behavior.

110. Why is praise for compliance important in classroom management? (Skill 9.3, Average Rigor)

A. Students will continue deviant behavior

B. Desirable conduct will be repeated

C. It reflects simplicity and warmth

D. Students will fulfill obligations

The correct answer is B: Desirable conduct will be repeated.

The tried-and-true principle that behavior that is rewarded will be repeated is demonstrated here. If other students laugh at a child's misbehavior, he will repeat it. On the other hand, if the teach rewards the behaviors she wants to see repeated, it is likely to happen.

111. When planning instruction, which of the following is an organizational tool to help ensure you are providing a well balanced set of objectives? (Skill 10.1, Rigorous)

A. Using a taxonomy to develop objectives

B. Determining prior knowledge skill levels

C. Determining readiness levels

D. Ensuring you meet the needs of diverse learners

Answer: A. Using a taxonomy to develop objectives

The use of a taxonomy, such as Bloom's, allows teachers to ensure the students are receiving instruction at a variety of different levels. It is important students are able to demonstrate skills and knowledge at a variety of different levels.

112. **When considering the development of the curriculum, which of the following accurately describe the four factors which need to be considered?**
(Skill 10.1, Rigorous)

A.   Alignment, Scope, Sequence, and Design

B.   Assessment, Instruction, Design, and Sequence

C.   Data, Alignment, Correlation, and Score

D.   Alignment, Sequence, Design and Assessment

Answer: A. Alignment, Scope, Sequence, and Design

When developing curriculum, it is important to first start with alignment. Alignment to state, national or other standards is the first step. Next, the scope of the curriculum involves looking at the amount of material covered within a grade level or subject. Next, the sequence of material needs to be considered. Finally, it is important to look at the design of the units individually from beginning to end.

113. **What do cooperative learning methods all have in common? (Skill 10.3, Rigorous)**

A. Philosophy

B. Cooperative task/cooperative reward structures

C. Student roles and communication

D. Teacher roles

Answer: B. Cooperative task/cooperative reward structures.

Cooperative learning situations, as practiced in today's classrooms, grew out of searches conducted by several groups in the early 1970's. Cooperative learning situations can range from very formal applications such as STAD (Student Teams-Achievement Divisions) and CIRC (Cooperative Integrated Reading and Composition) to less formal groupings known variously as "group investigation," "learning together," and "discovery groups." Cooperative learning as a general term is now firmly recognized and established as a teaching and learning technique in American schools. Since cooperative learning techniques are so widely diffused in the schools, it is necessary to orient students in the skills by which cooperative learning groups can operate smoothly, and thereby enhance learning. Students who cannot interact constructively with other students will not be able to take advantage of the learning opportunities provided by the cooperative learning situations and will furthermore deprive their fellow students of the opportunity for cooperative learning.

114. **What should be considered when evaluating textbooks for content? (Skill 10.3, Easy)**

A. Type of print used

B. Number of photos used

C. Free of cultural stereotyping

D. Outlines at the beginning of each chapter

The correct answer is C: Free of cultural stereotyping.

While textbook writers and publishers have responded to the need to be culturally diverse in recent years, a few texts are still being offered that don't meet these standards. When teachers have an opportunity to be involved in choosing textbooks, they can be watchdogs for the community in keeping the curriculum free of matter that reinforces bigotry and discrimination.

115. **Which of the following could be an example of a situation which could have an effect on a student's learning and academic progress? (Skill 11.1, Average Rigor)**

A.   Relocation

B.   Abuse

C.   Both of the Above

D.   Neither of the Above

Answer: C. Both of the Above

There are an unlimited amount of situations which can affect a student's learning. Teachers need to keep in mind this when teaching. Students are whole people and just as stress affects us as adults, children experience the same feelings. They usually do not have the same tool box that adults have to deal with the feelings and may require some additional guidance.

116. **Andy shows up to class abusive and irritable. He is often late, sleeps in class, sometimes slurs his speech, and has an odor of drinking. What is the first intervention to take?**
(Skill 11.1, Average Rigor)

A. Confront him, relying on a trusting relationship you think you have

B. Do a lesson on alcohol abuse, making an example of him.

C. Do nothing, it is better to err on the side of failing to identify substance abuse

D. Call administration, avoid conflict, and supervise others carefully.

The answer is D: Call administration, avoid conflict, and supervise others carefully.

Educators are not only likely to, but often do face students who are high on something. Of course, they are not only a hazard to their own safety and those of others, but their ability to be productive learners is greatly diminished, if not non-existent. They show up instead of skip, because it's not always easy or practical for them to spend the day away from home, but not in school. Unless they can stay inside they are at risk of being picked up for truancy. Some enjoy being high in school, getting a sense of satisfaction by putting something over on the system. Some just don't take drug use seriously enough to think usage at school might be inappropriate. The first responsibility of the teacher is to assure the safety of all of the children. Avoiding conflict with the student who is high and obtaining help from administration is the best course of action.